THE
HENLEY-ON-THAMES
BRANCH

AN ILLUSTRATED HISTORY OF

THE
HENLEY-ON-THAMES
BRANCH

BY

PAUL KARAU

WILD SWAN PUBLICATIONS LTD.

© Wild Swan Publications Ltd. and Paul Karau
ISBN 0 906867 03 7

FOR
REG DANIELLS

Designed by Paul Karau
Typesetting by Berkshire Publishing Services
Photo reproduction and offset plates by Oxford Litho Plates Ltd.
Printed in Oxford

Published by
WILD SWAN PUBLICATIONS LTD.
Hopgoods Farm Cottage, Upper Bucklebury, Berks.

—— CONTENTS ——

S. Fletcher

INTRODUCTION

Just before 6 p.m. there was hardly a soul to be seen at Henley station. The branch railcar was at Twyford and the numerous cars that religiously arrived to meet the London train had yet to appear. Inside, beneath the grimy timbers of the broad overall roof, lingered the ever present odour of burning lamp oil, and the usual gloom of the interior was pierced by the soft golden light of the evening sun penetrating through the skylight and side windows.

I was there each evening to witness the arrival of the London train, but soon came to realize that I derived at least as much pleasure from simply gazing around in anticipation — in fact just being there.

The long platforms stretching out into the sun were still equipped with rows of gas lamps whose decorative cast iron columns rose from mossy cracks between the paving slabs. Huge willows screened the railway from the riverside promenade, while on the opposite side the odd empty wagon lurked in the shade amidst the coaldust which carpeted the edge of the goods yard. The scene was one of tranquillity, a time for thought amidst the lengthening shadows cast by the romantic light and appropriately enhanced by evening birdsong.

This was not my first visit of the day as earlier on after school I had seen a friend, Michael Light, off on the train to Shiplake, but this second visit was really exciting as the London train invariably arrived in the charge of a 'Hall' or 'Castle' class engine — and there was always the possibility of being invited onto the footplate.

With the wind in the right direction it was often possible to hear the progress of the train coming down the branch, although its final appearance through Mill Lane bridge was quite unheralded as it coasted along the last stretch.

I was always pleased to stand in lone contemplation at the end of the platform and well remember the annoyance I felt when the spell was so abruptly broken by the arrival of the postman, with the wheels of his clattering trolley striking a regular beat over the joins in the paving as he came down the opposite platform. However, his presence was soon forgotten with the excitement of the train coming into view. As soon as it reached the end of the platform I turned and ran as fast as I could alongside the engine, watching the heavy connecting rod swing up and down to the beat of the vacuum pump as the huge iron wheels rolled along between the platform walls. As the tender brakes jarred, the loco finally came to rest and I was able to stare up into the cab while all the passengers hastened past clutching rolled umbrellas, newspapers and briefcases, totally preoccupied with making their way through the ticket barrier.

Some of the crews were not at all sympathetic to an enquiring schoolboy's face peering into their domain through the gap between the loco and tender, trying to catch a glimpse of the expiring fire, but to those who quite unofficially welcomed me aboard I truly owe my most treasured memories. The sheer excitement of climbing onto the footplate was as intense as the feeling of awe and intrusion once there. I always felt over-grateful and awkward about just where to stand to be the least possible trouble. Then, when the doors and windows of the train had been slammed shut and the left-over newspapers collected, we backed out into the sunlight with a sharp steady bark of exhaust as the coaches were propelled towards the carriage sidings.

To be on the footplate away from the station, overlooking the riverside meadows in the evening sun, was joy beyond belief, yet always too brief as the shunter worked quickly in detaching the stock and was soon hanging on the cab steps for a lift back to the station. We slowed past the signal box to hand over one or two of the evening papers and finally came to rest alongside the water tower. At the driver's suggestion, before leaving the engine I washed my hands with a grubby bar of soap and rinsed them in the bucket of warm water invariably standing in the corner, only to grip the same oily handrails on my descent from the cab.

I spent many such blissful evenings at the station, always greeted with a parting frown from the ticket collector as if to let me know that he knew where I'd been. But sadly the last night of regular steam-hauled London services remains only too vivid a memory. There was no ride for me then, just the unforgettable experience of realizing that as I peered over the iron railings from Cold Bath footpath with tears welling in my eyes, the Henley branch that I had come to know and love was lost for ever.

Paul Karau
Henley
1982

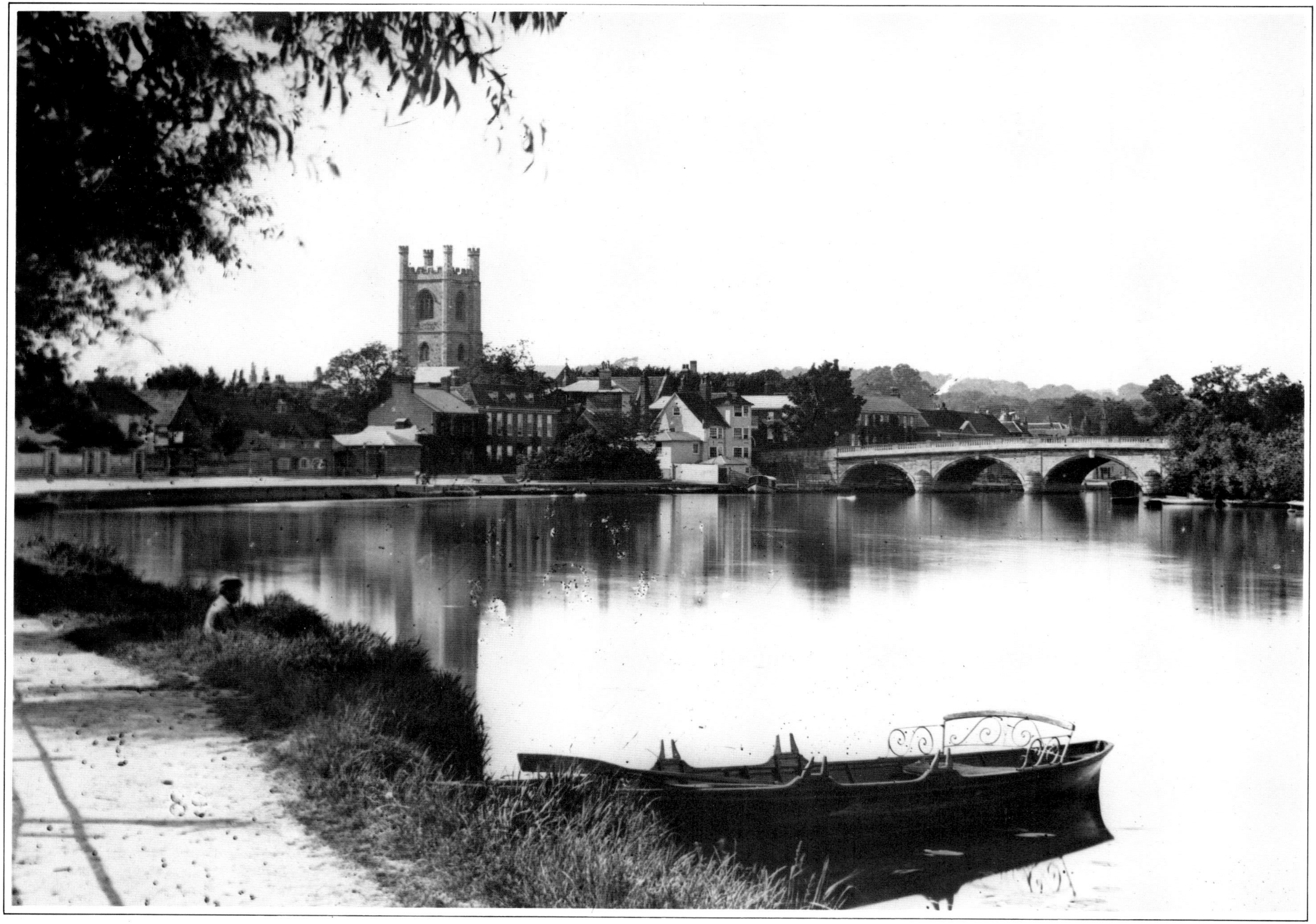

Geo. Bushell & Son

CHAPTER ONE

'A NEW ERA OF PROSPERITY'

THE town of Henley-on-Thames is situated in the southern corner of Oxfordshire alongside the River Thames. Although reputed to be one of the oldest towns in the county, the first positive documentary evidence for its existence occurs in 1149 and that only concerns the Manor of Henley. The church is first mentioned in 1204 and this rather late date, together with the long narrow property boundaries which are a feature of the older part of the town, apparently indicate that it was a new town created in the 12th century. The name is thought to mean 'at the high clearing' which may have referred to the manor site.

The familiar stone bridge over the Thames, linking Oxfordshire and Berkshire, was built in 1786 and replaced a badly damaged wooden bridge that had been partially swept away by the great flood of 1774. The new bridge was built to cope with the rapidly increasing traffic that was passing through Henley on the Great Western Road as a result of road improvements carried out by the local Turnpike Trusts.

At one time Henley was a prosperous agricultural market, with malting, lace-making and even glass-making industries. The river played a vital role in the town's economy, not only as a means of transporting local produce to London, but also because Henley became a terminal for the trans-shipment of goods between river and road. The large loop in the course of the river upstream from Henley, together with the difficulties in navigation before the replacement of the old flash locks, made the journey on to Wallingford both lengthy and costly. It was probably easier, therefore, to take goods on from Henley by road.

A weekly market was held in the town every Thursday, occupying the market place and Hart Street. Corn brought in from the surrounding area was sold for malting or grinding into flour or meal and much of this was sent to London by river. Sometimes 300 cart loads of corn or malt were sold on a single day, and in the 18th century the town was said to have been inhabited by 'mealmen, maltsters and bargemen', the latter taking corn and timber to London in barges.

The town was well served with coach services and in 1830 coaches from Holyhead, Shrewsbury, Worcester, Gloucester, Cheltenham, Stroud, Faringdon, Wantage, Oxford and Wallingford called at Henley, perhaps changing horses there at The Bell Inn or Red Lion. In addition, a number of passenger and freight services originated from the town.

The Great Western Railway had opened as far as Reading in March 1840, offering a new means of transport that was a vast improvement over existing road services, both in speed and comfort, and naturally drew considerable traffic. However, although intending railway travellers from Henley still had to make their way to Reading or Twyford stations, even after the introduction of omnibus services between Henley and Twyford in 1844, and later between Henley and Reading in 1847, perhaps surprisingly, Dixon's Henley to London coach was apparently still well patronised.

The earliest proposal for a railway that would have passed through Henley was that of the Tring, Reading and Basingstoke Railway conceived in 1833. The plans for this project were not, however, deposited for Parliamentary approval until 1845 by which time plans for three further schemes involving Henley had also been submitted. These were the South Midland and Southampton Railway, the Midland Grand Junction Railway and the Great Western Railway's own proposal for a branch line to Henley, a distance of some 4½ miles from the main line at Twyford.

Each of these schemes was rejected in Parliament, but the Great Western amended the plans for their own and made a second application the following year, this time with success, and the line was authorised on 22nd July, 1847.

During this period of 'railway mania', when numerous railway proposals were being made throughout the country, money was generally in short supply and the Great Western Railway found itself in financial difficulties. No construction work was therefore undertaken and the scheme was left in abeyance.

During the course of the GWR's opposition to the Mid-Western Railway in 1851, the company contended, as they had in 1847, that the district between Oxford and London was best served with branch lines from their own railway rather than a line passing through the midst of it. Although nothing had been done to further the Henley branch, at the beginning of 1852 the GWR resolved to obtain an extension of time for the construction of the branch as the powers granted in the existing Act were to expire in 1854.

Meanwhile, the inhabitants of Henley were growing anxious that the town should be served with rail communication and the Mayor accordingly convened a meeting for the purpose of considering the best means that could be adopted for introducing a railway to the town. Posters were displayed to advertise the meeting, which was held in the town hall on Thursday, 28th October, 1852.

The meeting was well attended and whilst Mr. Saunders, the secretary of the Great Western Railway, was unable to be present, he sent a communication to say that the railway was anxious to assist the inhabitants of Henley in constructing a branch line from Twyford to Henley. The

1

HENLEY RAILWAY.

PUBLIC MEETING

Having received a requisition numerously signed to convene a Meeting of the Inhabitants of this Town and Neighbourhood, for the purpose of considering the best means to be adopted for introducing a Railway into the Town.

I hereby *convene* a Meeting of the Inhabitants of this Town and Neighbourhood for the above purpose, to be held in the **TOWN HALL**, on **THURSDAY**, the **28**th of **OCTOBER** instant, at Three o'Clock in the Afternoon.

EDWARD YOUNG,

Mayor.

Henley, 16th October, 1852.

C. KINCH, PRINTER, HENLEY.

from direct Railway communication and stated that resolutions would be offered for the approval of the present meeting embodying the course considered most desirable to pursue to attain the object which he believed was almost unanimously desired.

Lord Camoys who rose to propose the first resolution read a communication he had received from Mr. Saunders, secretary to the Great Western Railway Company regretting he was unable to attend the meeting but stated that the Company was anxious to give every assistance to the inhabitants of Henley in making a branch line from thence to Twyford. His Lordship then read the following resolution which was seconded by W. B. Read Esq. and carried unanimously:—

> That it is the opinion of this meeting that the formation of a Railway is imperatively called for by the requirements of the town of Henley and the neighbourhood which has greatly suffered from the want of railway accommodation.

Colonel Knolly proposed the following resolution:—

> That a deputation from this meeting consisting of Lord Camoys, the Rev. Mr. Keene, the Mayor of Henley and Mr. Owthwaite attended by Mr. Cooper be requested to wait on the directors of the Great Western Railway Company to lay before them the inconvenience and injury sustained from the want of direct Railway communication and to urge them to carry out the powers which have already been granted to them by Parliament for that purpose.

Mr. Mercer seconded the resolution which was also carried.

Mr. Owthwaite moved the third resolution:—

> That in the meantime Mr. Cooper give such notices and adopt such preliminary proceedings as may be requisite to save the ensuing Session of Parliament.

meeting urged the company to carry out the powers already granted by Parliament and the following report appeared in *Jackson's Oxford Journal* on 30th October, 1852.

THE PROPOSED HENLEY RAILWAY

On Thursday afternoon the meeting called by the Mayor by Public Notice for the purpose of ascertaining the best means of providing the town with Railway accommodation was most numerously attended. A few minutes after 3 o'clock the Mayor attended by several gentlemen who have taken an active part in forwarding this object, entered the room and amongst those present were Lord Camoys, The Hon. T. Stonor, Colonel Knolly, C. Lane Esq., W. B. Reade Esq., J. F Hodges Esq., W. H. Brakspear Esq., T. S. Carter Esq., the Revds. C. E. R. Keene, H. Pechell, T. B. Morrell, C. Godby-Latter, Messrs. S. Cooper, J. Gwilts, N. Mercer & W. Jeston, R. Owthwaite, C. Norton, R. B. Child, J. Brooks and Z. Allnut, a considerable number of farmers and corn dealers, attendants of the Market with a great majority of the tradesmen of the town.

The Hon. T. Stonor proposed and W. H. Brakspear seconded that the Mayor should take the chair.

The Mayor in opening the business of the meeting remarked on the great advantages to be derived by such a town as Henley

This was supported by Mr. Jeston and also carried.

Mr. Lane remarked that he considered the meeting in this resolution was doing that which should be done by the Great Western Railway Company.

Lord Camoys explained that it was unavoidable for if time was expended in interview with the Company the period by which notice is required would probably have passed and the ensuing Session of Parliament be lost.

The Rev. T. B. Morrell proposed and Mr. Lane seconded a vote of thanks to the Mayor, who having replied, the meeting separated.

Charles Russell, Chairman of the GWR, received the deputation from the Railway Committee at Paddington the following week, the meeting also being attended by Brunel. The cost of the line was estimated at £45,000 and the outcome of the discussion was that the GWR would proceed with the line on the condition that the townspeople contributed £15,000 towards the cost, for which 3% per annum would be guaranteed together with a share of the profits.

When the Committee met on Thursday to receive the report of the deputation, a subscription list was opened

Henley Market Place and the old Town Hall.   *Courtesy Geo. Bushell & Son*

and half of the capital required was raised immediately in the room in £50 shares. As a result, the promoters were quite confident that the remainder of the shares would be taken up when made public.

It was suggested at the meeting that the line be diverted after crossing the Thames, to cross the turnpike road at Lashbrook and run to Henley on the west side of the river on higher ground, thus allowing the station to be built in the market place.

On Monday, 8th November, the shareholders met Mr. Murray, an engineer of the Great Western. He informed them that whilst the proposed diversion in the course of the railway was practicable, it could not be made without additional expense and delay in obtaining the necessary new Act.

The meeting was adjourned until Wednesday in order to obtain the opinion of the Board of Directors at Paddington. At this meeting it was agreed that notice be immediately given for the revival of the powers of the Act obtained in 1847 for the construction of the line surveyed and that the proposed deviation should not be attempted.

Accordingly a fresh Act of Parliament was secured, which received Royal Assent on 4th August, 1853, for reviving, extending and enlarging the powers conferred by the Act of 1847 and for raising additional capital.

The GWR prepared the plans for a single track branch line, built to the broad gauge of 7 ft. 0¼ ins. and at the same time made provision for possible future doubling of the branch by designing the overbridges to take double track formation. The company invited tenders for the line's construction in February, 1854, as follows:—

The Directors of the Great Western Railway Company will receive tenders for the construction of the Henley Branch of this Railway, a length of about 4½ miles. Drawings and specifications may be seen at the Engineers office, 18, Duke Street, Westminster on and after Monday the 27th instant. The tenders are to be addressed to the Directors of the Great Western Railway Company and delivered at their office at Paddington, before 12 o'clock on Wednesday the 22nd March next.

A meeting of subscribers to the projected railway was held on Saturday, 19th August, that year, and the proposals of the Great Western were laid before the meeting and unanimously accepted. The GWR optimistically undertook to finish the work by Christmas 1855 at the latest.

The plans of the line bear the name of Isambard Kingdom Brunel, who was, of course, still the Engineer of the Great Western Railway at the time. However, whilst he was responsible for the work, it is most likely, particularly by this time, that in practice either his chief assistant, T. H. Bertram, or Mr. Murray, was effectively the Engineer of the line.

On 12th December, 1853, a meeting of the parishioners of Shiplake took place at the Plough Inn (now the Plowden

Arms) to discuss the coming railway which was to cross their land. The line was to run through common land known as Lashbrook Green, the total length of the line through the parish of Shiplake being 1,534 yards. For this land the GWR agreed compensation of £249, which was eventually paid in 1856. The sum was divided as follows: £100 applied to the National School of the parish, £27 8s. 6d. to the owners of the land through which the line passed, and £16 13s. 4d. as compensation to the Lord of the Manor, the balance being applied towards the building of two new cottages on church land at Lashbrook, the rents from which were to be appropriated to Church expenses.

No references have been found of any ceremony of the turning of the first sod or, for that matter, the date when the construction of the line was actually started. However, in one of Brunel's reports that appeared in *Herepath's Railway Journal* for 13th February, 1855, he stated 'The Henley Branch is commenced and after winter will, I expect, proceed rapidly.'

Construction was hampered by a late fall of snow in February which rendered the roads impassable for a short period and snow drifts of up to nine feet in depth were reported in the locality. At the same time the omnibus that ran between Henley and the Great Western Railway at Twyford was compelled to suspend its journey for two days.

Details of the construction are obscure but it was not until the end of June that the seal of the company was affixed to the contract entered into with Mr. A. W. Ritson 'for the execution of the works on the Henley Branch'. In the same month Brunel reported 'The Henley Branch, on which the works are very light, is proceeding as fast as we may obtain occupation of the land and will not take long in executing'.

The Company's own forecast of the completion of the line before the end of 1855 was well short of the time actually required and by June the following year Brunel was still only able to put in his report, 'The Henley branch is in a forward state and no time will be lost in completing it.'

The authorised plans show the railway terminating at Friday Street, but, in the event, the site of the station was well short of the town, actually in the parish of Rotherfield Greys, the line terminating on a 10 acre plot selected by Brunel and purchased by the company from the trustees of the will of William Lamb. Much of the land, which extended to the Henley to Reading turnpike road, was never utilised by the railway and was resold in later years.

The two and a half years that it took to build the line appear to have been remarkably uneventful and the minute books only record one complaint. Mr. W. E. Saker, the tenant of Shiplake Mill, wrote to the company on 14th November 1855 to draw their attention to the increased floods at his mill caused by the piles supporting the bridge over the Thames. He also wrote to his MP and the matter was referred to Brunel.

Only one serious accident was reported during this time and this occurred on 2nd December, 1856, when James King, a labourer employed on the construction of the line, was killed by falling earth in a gravel pit.

By 1857 both the shareholders and the GWR were anxious that the line should be opened in time for the regatta that year. The company displayed great confidence and the *Oxford Journal* for 16th May announced that the railway was to be opened for passenger traffic on Monday, 1st June, with five trains each way per day. It also stated that the GWR intended to offer cheap fares by certain trains and in this respect the town would be placed on the same footing as Reading which would 'confer on the public an advantage beyond many expected to be derived from the completion of the railway'.

On 22nd April Brunel had written to the Board to enquire whether a refreshment room was required at Henley station as there was still time to introduce one in the plans. However, the directors decided this was unnecessary. No time was lost in commencing with the erection of the station buildings, but the following month while they were under construction and only the foundations laid for the turntable, the line had reached a sufficient stage of completion to enable the GWR to ask the Board of Trade to inspect the works in order that the line might be opened for the public.

Colonel Yolland carried out the inspection of the line for the Board on Monday, 25th May, and the contents of his report were as follows:

Sir,
    In compliance with the instructions contained in your letter of the 21st instant, I have this day inspected the Henley Branch of the Great Western Railway; and I have the honor to report, for the information of the Lords of the Committee of Privy Council for Trade, that, this Branch, which is single throughout, commences at the Twyford Station of the Great Western Railway, and ends at Henley a distance of 4 m. 46 chs.

With the exception of a long wooden viaduct, there are not any works of any magnitude on the Line which is a surface one, falling towards Henley with a ruling gradient of 1 in about 60.

The Land has been purchased, and the over bridges built, for a double line; but the under Bridges, Viaducts etc. have only been constructed for a single Line.

The line is laid down on the Broad Gauge of 7 ft. 0¼ ins., the rails made use of, being of the same form and weight as those on the Great Western Railway: viz: Bridge rails weighing 63 lbs per linear yard, placed on Longitudinal sleepers 13″ x 6½″ fastened with ¾ inch fang bolts. Transoms are placed 11 feet apart.

The width of the Line at formation level is 20½ feet in the Cuttings, and 23 feet on the embankments. The ballast is of good gravel 2 feet deep. Altogether the permanent way is in very good order, and the Line well finished off.

A separate platform for the Branch Trains clear of the Main Line has been erected at Twyford Station. There is however a sharp curve in the approach to this Station of 11 chains radius, which will require that Trains should approach at a slow speed.

There are four 'over' and one 'Under' Bridge — Two of the 'over' bridges have brick abutments and Iron Tops, one, a footbridge is of Timber: and all the other bridges are of brickwork — The whole are well built and sufficiently strong.

There are 3 Viaducts, all constructed of Timber, whose lengths are respectively 22, 310 and 90 yards: they are well constructed and amply strong.

There are no unauthorised level crossings on the Line.

The Stations on the line at the present time are Shiplake and Henley.

In making my Inspection, I noticed that the station buildings at Twyford, Shiplake and Henley were not complete and the platform at Shiplake also in an unfinished state. The foundations were in hand at Henley Station for an Engine Turntable but it will not probably be complete in less than a fortnight.

An additional signal is required at the Henley Station, which the Resident Engineer said should be immediately erected.

The Company are desirous of opening the Line on the 1st June; and I beg to recommend that their Lordships sanction may be given, provided the Great Western Railway Company will engage that only one Engine in steam shall be upon the Henley Branch Line at one and the same time, and that until the Engine Turntable is in working order, the Traffic may be solely worked by a Tank Engine.

Perhaps one of the most interesting facts revealed by the report is the description of the permanent way which evidently consisted of bridge rail mounted on longitudinal sleepers. The original plans for the line included a drawing of the permanent way showing Barlow laid directly to the ballast, but the Great Western experienced trouble with this method elsewhere on the system and presumably it was in the light of this that the company adopted the system described.

The first locomotive officially allocated to Henley was a 'Leo' class 2–4–0T named *Virgo*. This was shedded there for a full week before the line was opened and therefore presumably used to haul Colonel Yolland along the line for the purpose of his inspection. The loco is thought to have been used on the first public train and remained in service at Henley until the week ending 13th February the following year.

It is also possible that the first train may have been driven by William Mitchell, a driver who transferred from Wycombe when the line was opened, and thereafter remained on the branch as a regular driver for some years.

The branch was opened for public traffic on Monday, 1st June, and the event was celebrated by a public breakfast reported in *Jackson's Oxford Journal*:

OPENING OF THE HENLEY RAILWAY

On Monday last the branch railway from Twyford Station to this town was opened for public traffic, and the event was celebrated by a public breakfast at the Town Hall, at which some of the directors and chief officials of the Great Western Railway attended by invitation; the company numbered upwards of seventy persons, Lord Camoys presiding. Mrs. Williams of the Catherine Wheel Inn supplied the breakfast in her usual excellent style. Amongst the company besides the guests, were the Mayor (N. Mercer Esq.), C. Lane and J. Lane, Esqrs, the Rev. T. B. Morrell (Rector), Colonel Iredell, Lieut. Brooks, D. M. Gordon, P. B. Cooper, J. S. Burn, G. Pritt, A. Pritt, C. Dawson, W. H. Brakspear, S. Cooper, T. W. Jeston, J. Cooper, - Nind, C. Pennington, W. H. Workman, H. Stapleton, C. Plumbe, Esqrs., &c., &c.

After the customary loyal toasts were drunk, the Noble Chairman, in proposing the toast of the day, 'Success to the Henley Branch of the Great Western Railway' coupled with it 'The health of the Directors Present'. He remarked that it gave him great pleasure to attend the present meeting to celebrate the opening of a branch railway to connect the town with the main line of such a railway as the Great Western, and for which branch, without speaking slightingly of the exertions of the inhabitants, they were in great measure indebted to the directors of that company, who had, to effect the completion, met them more than half way, and although some little delay had occurred, the branch had been constructed in the very

superior manner discernible in all the works of the Great Western Railway Company; he trusted that the project would prove eminently successful, and he considered it was entitled to the support of the residents of the locality; the directors of a great commercial company like the Great Western had a two-fold object in view, that of giving satisfaction to the traveller and also of providing a dividend for the shareholder, which at times was difficult to carry out so as to receive the approbation of both parties, and occasionally a letter of complaint to the *Times* would ensue; yet on no line with which he was acquainted was so much comfort, convenience, civility and attention experienced as on the Great Western; it might be urged that from his frequently passing from Twyford to Paddington he was known, and therefore received more attention, but such was not the fact, as he found it equally a rule of conduct on the western portion of the line, where he was a stranger; he gave the directors great credit for their selection of officials, and he trusted this might be the commencement of a new era of prosperity to the inhabitants of the town of Henley, with whom he had long been intimately connected, and in whose welfare, he must be allowed to say, he always felt interested. It gave him great pleasure to be brought as he had been that morning, by a railway to the town, instead of having to travel through the mud or dust a distance of five miles of parish road from the Twyford station, and he was certain it would be the means of making numbers acquainted with the delightful scenery of the neighbourhood, to whom, but for this branch railway, it would never be known. – The toast was received with great applause, as were also his Lordship's remarks.

H. Simonds and - Ogilvie Esqrs., directors of the Great Western Railway, returned thanks.

The toast of 'Success to the Town of Henley' was replied to by the Mayor, who proposed 'The Health of the Chairman', which was received with great enthusiasm.

'The Rev. Mr. Morrell', 'The Mayor and Corporation, with thanks for the use of the Hall', 'Mr. Murray, engineer of the company', with other toasts, followed, and were duly acknowledged.

The Chairman then took back his departure, stating that several of the guests had expressed a desire to see something of the town, &c., to which this was their first visit.

The trains on Monday (of which there are six each way daily) were tolerably well patronized, and the station during the whole of the day was the scene of much life and bustle; the church bells rang merrily throughout the day, and contributed in giving a holiday feature to the occasion.

The opening of the line naturally made connecting services to Twyford redundant and consequently the four-horse coach, which had to run twice daily between the Red Lion Hotel and Twyford to take passengers wishing to join the Great Western Railway at Twyford station, made its last journey on this day.

The line was opened well in time for the 1857 regatta which was held during the week ending 27th June, and Brunel was able to report on the 30th of the month that the Henley line was now in good working order in every respect, and in fact this half yearly report was the last signed by him as his health was failing. He died two years later at the age of 53.

The line had taken some 2½ years to complete, more than double the time anticipated, the eventual cost totalling some £79,000, again well in excess of the figure first quoted. Conversely in January 1858 the GW minute books record a total subscription from the townspeople of only £9,575 – below two-thirds of that pledged.

HENLEY STATION c.1860. *Taken from an original painting by Sean Bolan.*

CHAPTER TWO

THE BROAD GAUGE

1857-76

THE GWR main line was opened to passengers as far as Twyford on 1st July 1839 and this remained as a terminus for some nine months while the section to Reading, which included the impressive Sonning Cutting, was completed. The original station was equipped with a low wooden station building, 'T' shaped in plan with hipped roofs and situated on the north side of the line. The main part of the building was a shelter open towards the rails and enclosing a 3 ft. high timber platform, along the edge of which were timber columns supporting the roof. It was enclosed at the rear and presumably entered via the offices that connected at right angles to it. The track plan below shows a large building spanning the lines. This originally formed an overall roof cum stock shed (with doors) between the passenger platforms of the original station at Maidenhead. However, when the line was extended, it was re-erected at Twyford, again for stock storage.

No doubt 'Twyford Depot', as it was referred to on the original drawings, was primarily concerned with the forwarding of supplies and materials for the ongoing construction work. The GWR provided a connecting coach service to ferry passengers between Twyford and

Reading and at least three other carriers operated similar services. With all this activity and the excitement and wonder at being able to reach London in little more than an hour, it is not difficult to imagine the transformation the railway had brought about to this sleepy little community.

The main line was opened through to Reading in March 1840 but it was not until 1845 that the handsome brick and stone station buildings and (in this instance staggered) platforms that we associate with Brunel's broad gauge, finally replaced the temporary wooden structures. It also appears that one of the familiar Gothic style goods sheds was also built at Twyford at the same time. This is featured in the illustration overleaf.

The construction of the Henley branch later disrupted the 'clean' simple layout of the station at Twyford. The site of the new branch junction was unfortunate in relation to the station's design at this time in that the branch left the main line alongside the existing goods yard and ran right through the same, not only severely restricting the accommodation of the yard, but also dividing it. The deposited plans show that it was originally intended to take the branch off the main line

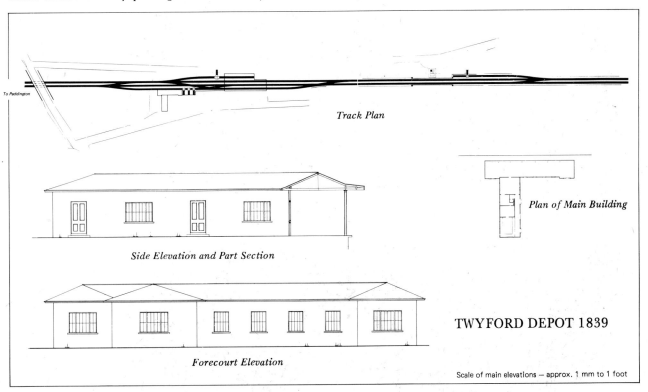

To Paddington

Track Plan

Plan of Main Building

Side Elevation and Part Section

TWYFORD DEPOT 1839

Forecourt Elevation

Scale of main elevations — approx. 1 mm to 1 foot

immediately to the west of the existing goods shed. However, in the event, it appears that the new junction layout necessitated the removal of the building and in its place a timber-built goods shed was erected in 1857 a little further to the west. This new structure was less striking in design but, curiously, whilst the original plans for Henley include a timber-built goods shed, it was a red brick Gothic style building that materialised. Whether this incorporated any of the masonry from the Twyford building is unknown but the coincidence does not preclude this. If this was the case per-haps as the divided goods yard at Twyford was so far from satisfactory, a more temporary timber building was the obvious choice and Henley the more suitable site for the more permanent and prestigious design.

TWYFORD STATION c.1850. *From Measom's Guide.*

What is certain is that the resulting goods yard at Twy-ford presented a danger to local traders and railway staff making their way across the line to the goods shed. Even the new passenger platform was, in effect, built in this yard and the local coal merchant, John Marshall of Reading, had lost his tenancy of a wharf on land required for the branch.

There were no run-round facilities alongside the new platform and some doubt is cast as to whether the loop beyond the platforms was used for that purpose. Certainly in early standard gauge days, the branch coaches were shunted using a chain, as mentioned in the accident des-cribed on page 20. The branch was connected to the main line by means of a single trailing connection with the 'up' main line, 'down' trains having to reverse onto the 'up' line to gain access to the branch. This arrangement, which avoided facing points, lasted until at least 1884 and probably until the 1892 re-development of the station. Incidentally, the signalman's shelter at this time was des-cribed by a station master as a 'signalman's kennel' in which there was barely room for two people to stand.

The following notes may help to highlight some aspects of the appearance of the young branch line although a more detailed route descrip-tion in later years is given in Chapter Five. The single line formation and broad gauge track undoubtedly presented a very different scene to that which evolved in later years.

The journey over the greater part of the route to Henley was uninterrupted as Shiplake was the only inter-

TWYFORD STATION c.1865. *An impression by Sean Bolan.*

mediate station on the line at this time. The recent earth works, post and rail fencing and young bushes must have presented quite a stark appearance compared with the way that the line nestles into its surroundings today and there were only two overbridges between Twyford and Shiplake.

The line was carried across the River Thames by an extensive timber viaduct and, just before Shiplake station, across Lashbrook by another similar timber structure. Shiplake was served by a minor wayside station which stood amidst fields away from the village proper. A small wooden station building stood on the short platform at the far end of which the line crossed a quiet lane leading from the village down to the river. The siding here was provided in 1859 at the expense of a Mr. Lakes. He used it to load certain unspecified 'first class goods' which were conveyed to Paddington at a rate of one shilling per ton. The public could also use this facility, the income derived (6d per ton) being applied 'in diminution of the debt for making it'.

Further on at the level crossing where the railway crossed Mill Lane on the approach to Henley, was another isolated spot where the red brick crossing keeper's house stood alone, overlooking the surrounding meadows. Mill Lane then served New Mills which produced paper and corn and was situated on the west bank of the river opposite Marsh Mill.

No track plans of Henley station in Broad Gauge days are now believed to exist and even the first Ordnance Survey was carried out just after the line was converted. However, it seems likely that the plan was little different to the standard gauge layout of 1876.

Little evidence remains to record the operation of the line at this time. By 1867 it was worked with a train staff and regulated by Spagnoletti's disc block telegraph (introduced on the GWR in 1863), the instruments presumably being housed in the station buildings as signal boxes are not believed to have been provided until the early 1870s.

Although details of these early years are scarce, the locomotives allocated to Henley, from the opening of the line to the beginning of the 1860s, were as follows:

As already mentioned, *Virgo* the first locomotive allocated to Henley, was a 'Leo' class 2—4—0T. The loco was designed by Gooch and built by Rothwell and Co. of Bolton in 1841 as an outside sandwich-framed 2—4—0 which had been converted to a saddle tank to increase adhesive weight. This loco was supplemented by 'Firefly' class 2—2—2T *Falcon* during the 14 day period ending 10th October and the 26 day period ending 31st December, 1857. Subsequent allocations were as follows:

Period	Ending	Locos
28 days	13th March 1858	*Vulcan* (unclassified 2—2—2T)
28 days	10th April 1858	*Vulcan* and *Arrow* ('Firefly' class 2—2—2T)

MILL LANE CROSSING c.1865. *An impression by Sean Bolan.*

56 days	5th June	1858	*Vulcan*
25 days	20th June	1858	*Vulcan* and *Gazelle* ('Sun' class 2—2—2T)
27 days	17th July	1858	*Vulcan*
28 days	14th Aug.	1858	*Vulcan* and *Gazelle*
35 days	18th Sept.	1858	*Vulcan* and *Aeolus* (unclassified 2—2—2T)
28 days	16th Oct.	1858	*Aeolus*
56 days	11th Dec.	1858	*Aeolus* and *Gazelle*
20 days	31st Dec.	1858	*Aeolus*
50 days	19th Feb.	1859	*Aeolus* & *Lance* ('Sun' class 2—2—2T)
28 days	19th March	1859	*Antelope* ('Sun' class 2—2—2T)
28 days	16th April	1859	*Antelope* & *Djerid* ('Sun' class 2—2—2T)
56 days	11th June	1859	*Antelope*
19 days	30th June	1859	*Antelope* & *Djerid*
51 days	20th Aug.	1859	*Antelope*
133 days	31st Dec.	1859	*Antelope* & *Djerid*
105 days	14th April	1860	*Antelope*
28 days	12th May	1860	*Antelope*, *Lance* ('Sun' class) & *Snake* (unclassified)
70 days	21st July	1860	*Snake* & *Viper* (both unclassified)
28 days	18th Aug.	1860	*Snake*, *Sun* ('Sun' class) & *Viper*
84 days	10th Nov.	1860	*Snake* & *Sun*
51 days	31st Dec.	1860	*Snake*
19 days	19th Jan.	1861	*Snake* & *Eagle* (unclassified 2—2—2)
28 days	16th Feb.	1861	*Sun* & *Eagle*
28 days	16th March	1861	*Sun*, *Eagle* & *Snake*
21 days	19th July	1862	*Eagle*, *Lynx*, ('Firefly' class) & *Vulcan*

Jan. 1858
Public Timetable

HENLEY BRANCH. *Passengers between London and Henley Branch will have to Change Carriages at Twyford.*

Distance	DOWN. Starting from	Week Days 1 Class 1 & 2	2 Class 1, 2, 3	3 Class 1 & 2	4 Class 1 & 2	5 1 & 2 Class	6 Class 1 & 2	7 Class 1 & 2	8 Class 1 & 2	9 Class 1 & 2	Sundays 1 Class 1, 2, 3	2 Class 1 & 2	3 Class 1 & 2	4 Class 1 & 2
		a.m.	a.m.	a.m.	p.m.	..	p.m.	p.m.	p.m.	...	a.m.	a.m.	p.m.	p.m.
	London (Pad. Sta.)	..	7 20	10 0	1 0	.	4 0	5 30	7 0	.	8 0	.	2 0	7 0
30¾	Twyford arr.	...	8 52	11 10	2 7	..	5 12	6 46	8 16	..	9 35	...	3 10	8 20
—	Twyford dep.	7 37	9 0	11 15	2 15	..	5 15	6 50	8 20	...	9 40	.	3 15	8 25
33¼	Shiplake	7 44	9 8	11 23	2 23	..	5 23	6 58	8 28	...	9 48	...	3 23	8 33
35¼	Henley	7 50	9 15	11 30	2 30	...	5 30	7 5	8 35		9 55	.	3 30	8 40

Distance from Henley	UP. Starting from	Week Days 1 Class 1, 2, 3	2 Class 1 & 2	3 Class 1 & 2	4 Class 1 & 2	5 Class 1 & 2	6 Class 1, 2, 3	7 Class 1 & 2	8 Class 1 & 2	Sundays 1 Class 1 & 2	2 Class 1 & 2	3 Class 1, 2, 3	4 Class 1 & 2
		a.m.	a.m.	a.m.	p.m.	...	p.m.	p.m.	p.m.	a.m.	a.m.	p.m.	p.m.
0	Henley	7 20	8 0	10 40	12 55	...	3 0	6 25	7 20	8 0	..	2 50	5 5
2	Shiplake	7 26	8 6	10 46	1 1	...	3 6	6 31	7 26	8 6	...	2 56	5 10
4½	Twyford	7 33	8 15	10 55	1 10	..	3 15	6 40	7 35	8 14	.	3 5	5 20
4½	Twyford	7 35	8 22	11 8	1 15	..	3 18	...	7 37	8 15	...	3 10	5 22
35¼	London (Pad. Sta.)	8 55	9 40	12 30	2 25	...	4 55	...	9 0	9 30	..	5 0	6 40

1868 Service Timetable

HENLEY BRANCH.

Down. Twyford to Henley. Week Days.

Dist.	Single Line.	1 Pass.	2 Pass.	3 Pass.	4	5 Pass.	6 Pass.	7 Pass.	8 GOODS	9 Pass.	10	11	12
		a.m.	a.m.	a.m.		p.m.	p.m.	p.m.	p.m.	p.m.			
	Twyford dp	7 50	8 50	11 30	.	2 0	4 25	6 40	7 35	8 35	.	.	.
2¾	Shiplake ..	8 0	9 0	11 40	..	2 10	4 35	6 50	—	8 45	..	..	..
4½	Henley ar.	8 5	9 5	11 45	...	2 15	4 40	6 55	7 50 R	8 50	...	...	...

Down. Twyford to Henley. Sundays.

Dist.	STATIONS.	1 Pass.	2	3 Pass.	4 Pass.	5 Pass.	6	7	8	9	10	11	12
		a.m.		p.m.	p.m.	p.m.							
	Twyford dp	10 23	.	3 47	6 3	8 35	.	.	.	.	.	.	.
2¾	Shiplake ..	10 33	..	3 57	6 13	8 45	..	..	..	..	..	...	..
4½	Henley ar.	10 38	...	4 2	6 18	8 50	...	...	...	...	...	.	...

This Line is worked by Train Staff between Twyford and Henley. R To run when required only.

Up. Henley to Twyford. Week Days.

Dist.	Single Line.	1 Pass.	2 Pass.	3 Pass.	4 Pass.	5	6 Pass.	7	8 Ps & Gds	9 GOODS	10 Pass.	11	12
		a.m.	a.m.	a.m.	p.m.		p.m.		p.m.	p.m.	p.m.		
	Henley dp	7 5	8 25	10 40	1 25	.	3 15	.	6 0	6 55	8 0	.	.
1¾	Shiplake ..	7 10	8 30	10 45	1 30	..	3 20	..	6 5	—	8 5	..	..
4½	Twyford ar.	7 20	8 38	10 55	1 40	...	3 30	...	6 15	7 10 R	8 15	...	...

Up. Henley to Twyford. Sundays.

Dist	STATIONS.	1 Pass.	2	3 Pass.	4 Pass.	5 Pass.	6	7	8	9	10	11	12
		a.m.		p.m.	p.m.	p.m.							
	Henley dp	8 45	.	1 45	5 30	8 5	.	.	.	.	.	.	.
1¾	Shiplake ..	8 50	..	1 50	5 35	8 10	..	..	..	..	..	..	..
4½	Twyford ar.	9 0	...	1 58	5 45	8 20	...	...	...	...	...	...	...

R. To run when required only.

Vulcan as a 2–2–2T. *British Railways*

We are fortunate in having an insight into a few of the incidents that took place at Twyford between September, 1865, and the following March, through the eyes of Hubert A. Simmons, station master at Twyford, whose recollections were published under a pen name in a book entitled *Memoirs of a Station Master* by Ernest Struggles.

One of the incidents involved a mother and her son who were travelling together from Reading to Henley. It seems that at Reading the son was told that Henley was the second stop and so did not expect to alight at the first. At Twyford it was the custom for the porters to call out 'Twyford! Change for Shiplake and Henley'. Consequently, when the son heard this he conferred with a fellow passenger and got out of the train with a large hamper as quickly as he could, just as the train was pulling away from the station. He fell on to the platform and was unable to help his mother who, in trying to follow, fell behind the carriage in which she was travelling and under the train. She was taken to the Station Hotel but died fifteen minutes later. This accident has been traced in the *Berkshire Chronicle* where it was reported to have occurred on Monday, 11th September, 1865. The deceased was Hannah Smith, a 66 year old widow.

The following accident does not appear to have been reported in the local press and therefore remains undated. According to Mr. Simmons, the station master at Henley at the time was extremely inefficient and as a result of repeated complaints was visited by Mr. Bessant, the District Superintendent. Mr. Simmons was invited to accompany Mr. Bessant on his visit to Henley and in order that the Superintendent could catch a certain train home from Twyford, they returned from Henley on a light engine.

The meeting at Henley was a stormy one and the engine driver was unhappy at having to wait for them. The atmosphere seems to have persisted throughout the journey and as they slowed down on their approach to Twyford, the goods train, by which Mr. Bessant wished to travel, arrived. 'What do you want to shut off steam for?' said Mr. Bessant to the driver. 'Do you want me to miss that train?' 'You can have more steam if you like it' growled the driver, who apparently then used enough steam to convince Mr. Simmons that he would not be able to pull up short of a horse box that was standing in front of the buffers. The two passengers jumped to safety, leaving the crew on the loco 'which having cannoned the horse box, drove it with one jump into the pocket of the first class waiting-room through the window, and then re-charging, the engine took the corner of the station, a stone building, and misplaced a large portion of masonry.' Fortunately no-one was hurt.

The first member of the Royal Family to travel over the line is believed to have been the Prince of Wales who apparently rode on a regular service train. The Prince arrived at Henley station shortly before 4.00 p.m. on Sunday, 11th March, 1866, and was on his way to Shirburn Castle for a meeting of the South Oxfordshire Hounds the following morning. He was expected to return by the 5.55 p.m. train the following day. Many people assembled at the station to witness his departure but were disappointed as, in the event, the Prince returned via the Thame branch to London.

The majority of railways in other parts of the country were laid to the standard gauge of 4 ft. 8½ ins. and with the obvious inconvenience of transferring goods from wagons of one gauge to another, the fate of Brunel's Broad Gauge was inevitable. Conversion of the system to standard gauge had already been decided upon and the conversion of existing railways was already under way when in 1872 the residents of Henley complained of the inconvenience caused by the trans-shipment of goods. The Henley branch was still broad gauge and on the 11th June a letter from the inhabitants of Henley and district was sent to the Great Western requesting that the Henley branch should be converted and enclosing a petition to the same effect.

Henley-on-Thames
May 1872

To The Directors of The Great Western Railway

Gentlemen,
We the undersigned inhabitants of Henley & the Neighbourhood beg respectfully to call your attentions to the very great inconvenience we are subjected to by the break of gauge to this place from the Main line.
The delay in the transit of our goods, arising from the necessity of transfer from Narrow to Broad gauge trucks,

The timber viaduct over the Thames.   *British Railways*

HENLEY BRANCH
GREAT WESTERN RAILWAY.
THAMES VIADUCT .

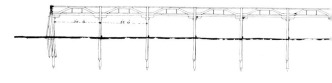

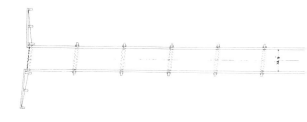

Elevation of Trusses A and B.

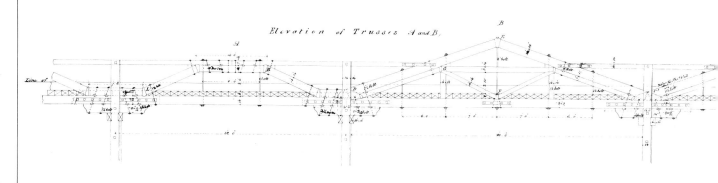

Plan

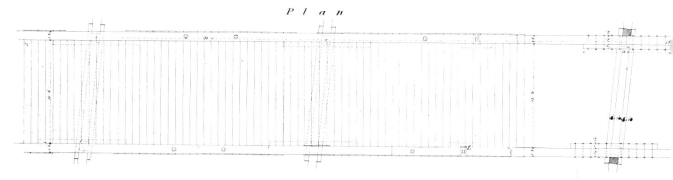

Transverse Section
(32 Ft Truss.)

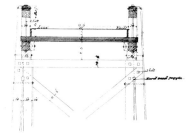

Transverse Section
(of Truss C)

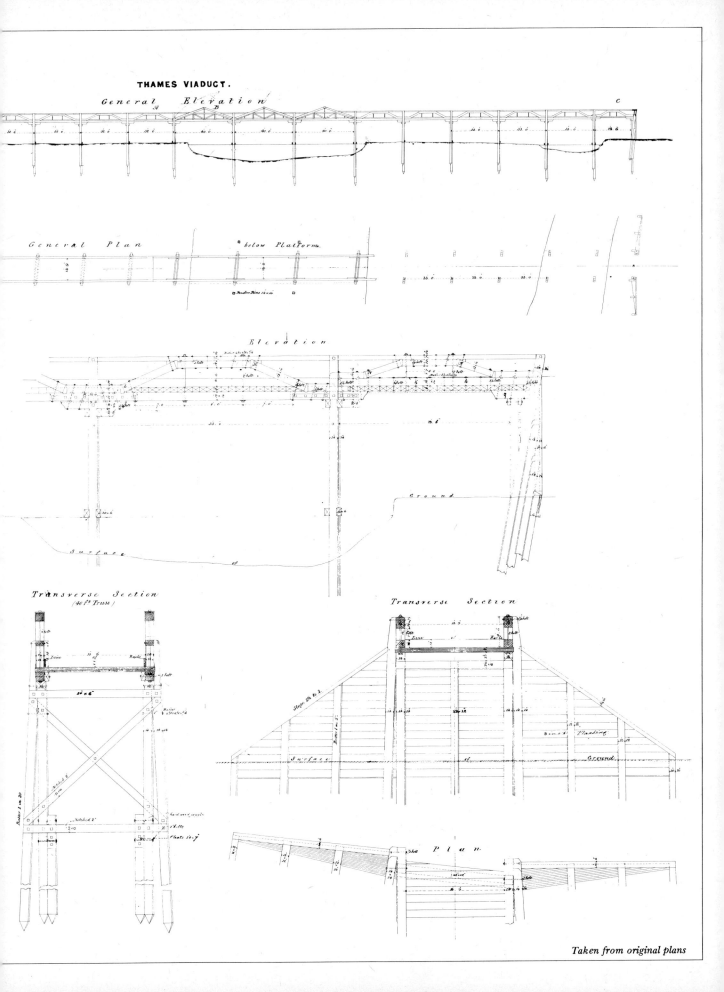

THAMES VIADUCT.

General Elevation

General Plan below Platform.

Elevation

Transverse Section
(40 ft Truss)

Transverse Section

Plan

Taken from original plans

G.W.R. HENLEY BRANCH

Foot Bridge at 3 Mls 26 Chs.

Transverse Section at A B

Section at CD

Elevation.

Plan of Superstructure

Plan (planking removed)

Taken from original plans

Flood Arches at 1 M^ls 75 Ch^s

G.W.R. HENLEY BRANCH

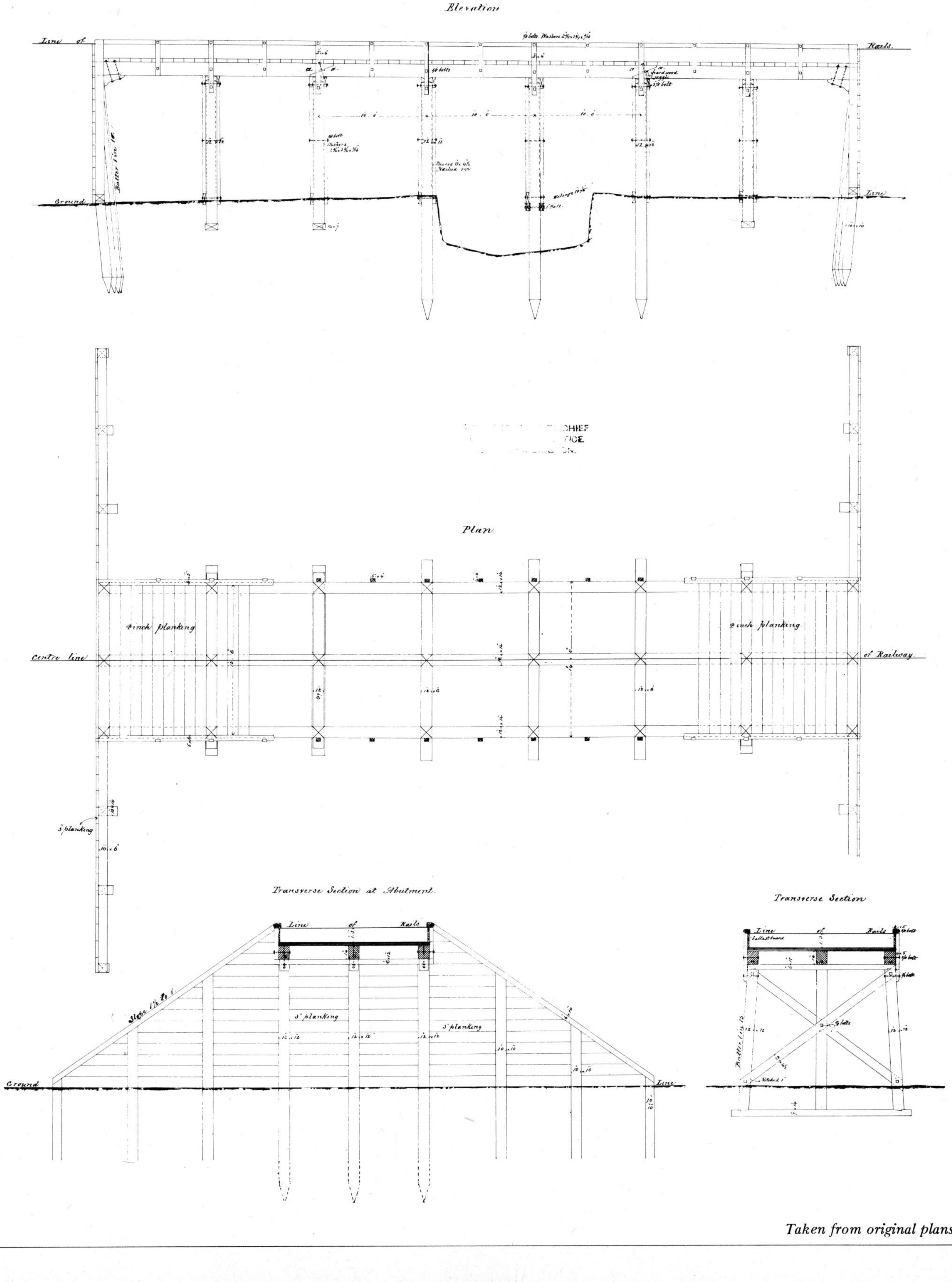

Elevation
Line of Rails
Ground Line
10.0
10.0
10.0
Batter 1 in 16
Plan
4 inch planking
4 inch planking
Centre line of Railway
3 planking
10 x 6
Transverse Section at Abutment
Line of Rails
Slope 1½ to 1
3" planking
3" planking
Ground
Line
Transverse Section
Line of Rails
Ballast board
Batter 1 in 15
Ground

Taken from original plans

which is often the cause of their sustaining considerable damage compels us to request you to take into your favourable consideration the speedy alteration of the gauge to this town in order that the loss and inconvenience we have now to complain of may be removed.

This letter seems to have had no effect at all in hastening the conversion as, in the event, of the lines that belonged to the company at the time, the Henley branch was to become the last to be converted. The Great Western was already committed with similar work elsewhere and considerably later, in August 1875, it was reported that with the exception of the Henley branch, the narrow gauge had been laid on all lines belonging to the company, and that as far as the Great Western were concerned, the broad gauge had to be maintained only for through traffic with companies west of Bristol.

The Henley branch was finally converted on Friday, 24th March, 1876, and at that time was the quickest conversion of all. The line was in the hands of the engineers from 9.30 p.m. that day until 9.30 a.m. the following morning and only two passenger trains were suspended.

Mr. R. M. Parkinson, a civil engineer who spent the first four years of his career in the service of the Great Western, later recalled his experience of the occasion and

the following extract appeared in the *Great Western Railway Magazine* in December 1941:

In the following March I found myself at nine o'clock one evening in the company of two permanent-way inspectors in a packer's hut midway between Twyford and Henley. The slopes of the railway were covered with men, but all one could hear was the distant sound of an engine shunting in Henley station yard. At length there came a whistle and we could hear the approaching train, followed by a kind of roar which developed into, 'Now, all together, over,' with a grunt like a miner's, when he brings his sledge down on the drill.

Directly the train had passed, every one was alive. Each inspector had four gangs of five and twenty men in his mile. Two of the twenty-five went ahead knocking out the fastening, two pairs followed cutting the transoms which had already been marked, and two more followed the main gang refixing the bolts and straps. By midnight the line on our two miles had been slewed in from 7 ft. 0¼ in. to the 4 ft. 8½ in. gauge, and we retired to our hut to feed and, as we hoped, to sleep. But not so; one of the inspectors, being of the opinion that if we did not keep awake we should catch cold, threw a fog signal into the fire and we promptly moved out. I then walked towards Twyford, where progress had been slower, as the line was curved and the rails had to be cut in many places. At 4 a.m. we were about again, but there was not sufficient light for an hour to lift and pack the rails, though we managed to get a train through by eight o'clock.

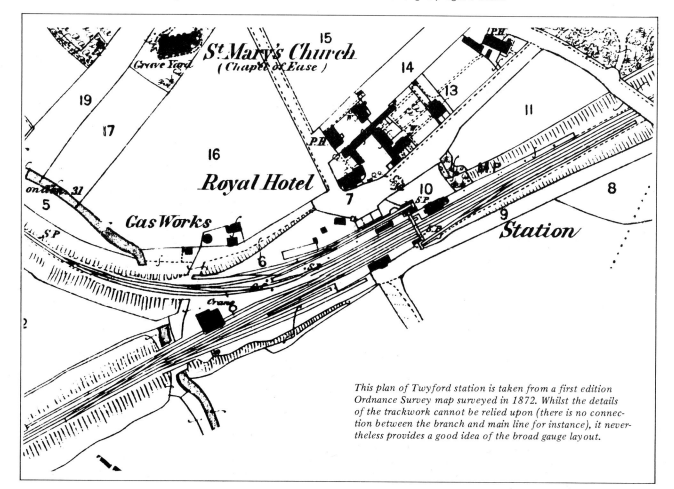

This plan of Twyford station is taken from a first edition Ordnance Survey map surveyed in 1872. Whilst the details of the trackwork cannot be relied upon (there is no connection between the branch and main line for instance), it nevertheless provides a good idea of the broad gauge layout.

CHAPTER THREE

IMPROVING THE LINE

1876-1904

SURPRISINGLY, the Board of Trade inspection following the gauge conversion did not take place until 2nd February 1877. On reading the subsequent report it appears that the inspecting officer, Colonel Yolland, was a firm believer in the stability of the broad gauge. This opinion is apparent in his criticism of the level crossing at Mill Lane where the original gates closed across the road but not completely across the railway. He states that 'this was not of so much importance while the Branch Line was a Broad Gauge Line, as there is no instance that I know of, of a Broad Gauge train being thrown off the rails when running over Horses or Cattle — but on Narrow Gauge lines very serious Accidents have frequently resulted from Horses and Cattle straying on to Lines and being run over, and throwing trains off the line.' He therefore stipulated that the gates should alternately close across the road and rail.

Signalling in connection with the 'long siding' off the 'up' main line at Twyford was also criticised. Stranded wire, operating bolt locking on the points of the through crossing, was to be replaced with rodding, and the rails on the sharp curve leaving Twyford station (which were fitted with a check rail by this time) were also in need of renewal. At Shiplake either the rails of one of the catchpoints on the loop line were to be extended and 'turned' up' (to prevent an engine which might have overrun from falling down the bank into a 'pool of water') or, as happened, the ground was to be filled in and levelled. The Colonel also decided that a railing was required along the back of the platform 'to prevent people from falling off it'!

At Henley his criticisms were confined to an alteration in the interlocking of sundry levers in the signal box, but elsewhere he was generally concerned with the state of

The 'Flying Dutchman' speeding through Twyford on the broad gauge c.1885.
Marsh Bros., Henley

repair of the post and rail fencing and also mentioned that the brickwork of the bridges was in need of repointing. The report also mentions that the wooden viaducts were undergoing repair at the time.

It was not until the beginning of the 1890s that any further development of significance seems to have taken place on the branch. However, one minor change that immediately followed the gauge conversion, the stopping up of a footpath at Henley station, was to give the company greater freedom in the later development of the site.

In August 1876 the company received an application for them to dedicate to the public a portion of the station approach road at Henley. The directors agreed to this providing the local authorities would agree to the closing of certain footpaths crossing the railway's line and land near the station, and also provided the roadway was widened and improved and the turntable removed.

The footpath that crossed the neck of the yard at Henley station had obviously become impractical for smooth operation when so many traffic movements were hindered by the inconvenience caused by members of the public maintaining their right of way over the running lines. Consequently, the railway obtained the necessary powers to stop up this path together with another that led from the Henley to Shiplake turnpike road to the approach road at the north-western end of the terminus.

An 1876 plan of the station at this time shows a third exit from the turntable which avoided the overall roof and ran along the eastern side of the station, past the engine shed, thus forming an additional loop line. This loop, which was inherited from the broad gauge layout, was converted to a siding (slewed away from the turntable) to serve a new coal wharf for Messrs. R. Toomer & Co. This

HENLEY-ON-THAMES 1876 standard gauge track plan

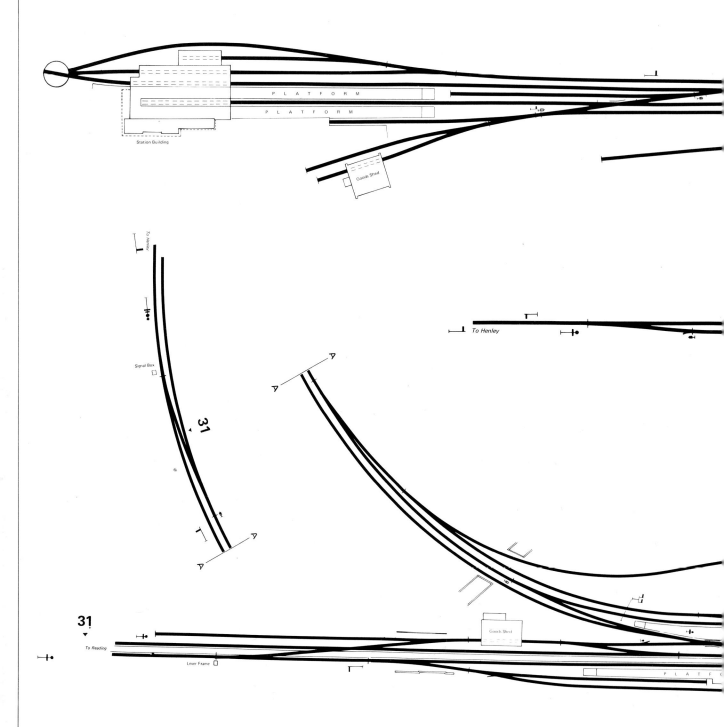

Station Building

P L A T F O R M

P L A T F O R M

Goods Shed

To Henley

Signal Box

31

To Henley

31

To Reading

Lever Frame

Goods Shed

P L A T F O

TWYFORD 1876 mixed gauge track plan

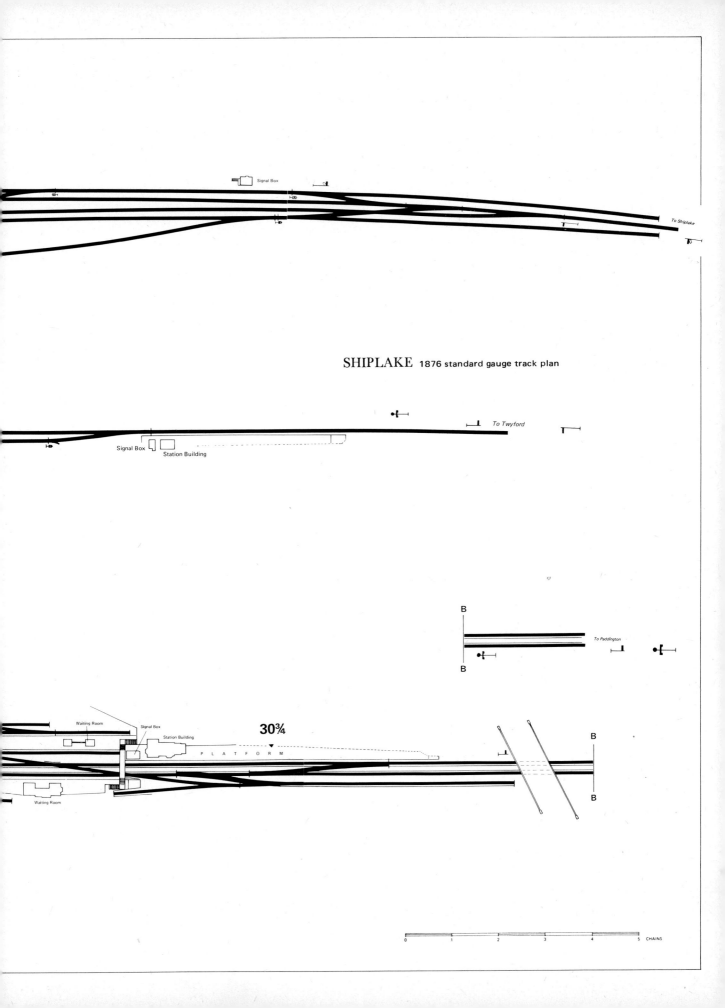

SHIPLAKE 1876 standard gauge track plan

Signal Box

To Shiplake

To Twyford

Signal Box
Station Building

B

To Paddington

B

Waiting Room

Signal Box

Station Building

30¾

P L A T F O R M

B

B

Waiting Room

B

0   1   2   3   4   5 CHAINS

Mr. Davis' new roller mill.   *Author's collection*

company paid a rent of £30 per annum for the accommodation and built an office and weighbridge on the land
leased to them.

In 1878 a private siding was also laid to serve Davis'
flour mill at Twyford, and for many years most of their
corn and flour traffic was carried by rail.

There had been a water mill at Twyford since at least
as long ago as 1363. Silk weaving was carried out until
1829, when the factory was disposed of, the hand looms
being unable to compete with more advanced machinery
introduced elsewhere. In its place a substantial flour mill
was constructed, driven by water and steam, a great deal
of it being built by Lawrence Davis in 1869. After his
death in 1886 at the early age of 42, his widow took over
the ownership of the business.

A fire occurred at the mill during the early morning of
Tuesday, 22nd December, 1891, apparently caused by the
overheating of a bearing. The Twyford volunteer fire
brigade attended and were helped by local villagers. Tele-
graphs were sent to the neighbouring fire brigades at
Reading and Maidenhead via the railway telegraph at the
signal box, which at that time was the quickest means of
sending for help in such an emergency.

The blaze lasted for twelve hours but the Maidenhead
brigade did not reach Twyford until long after their
Reading colleagues, only to find that their services were
not required. The former owner of the mill, the late Mr.
Lawrence Davis, was in fact the founder of the local volunteer fire brigade and, until his death, its captain.

A new roller mill was designed by Mr. L. Davis and
built 10 months after the fire. The new structure was
designed to minimise fire risk as much as possible. It was
powered by water but was also equipped with a 60 h.p.
horizontal condensing steam engine which was used as

auxiliary power when there was insufficient water. The
April 1893 issue of *The Miller* praised the new mill and
said 'The flour as might be expected in such a mill is of
super excellent quality'.

The divided goods yard at Twyford that resulted
from the course taken by the new branch line was most
unsatisfactory. It appears that the GWR first decided to
acquire additional land for a new yard further to the west,
between the branch curve and the River Loddon, as early
as 1865 but it was not until 1892 that the new yard was
actually under construction.

In May, during the construction of the new goods shed,
a lad named William Carter was knocked down by the
Henley branch train while it was being shunted. The engine
and carriages were not on the same line at the time, the
carriages being drawn along with a chain. The boy was
crossing the line and, not realising this, stepped clear of
the engine and in front of the coaches which knocked him
over. He later died in Reading hospital.

When Twyford station was first built there was no
station footbridge but one was provided when it became a
junction in 1857. Besides connecting the 'up' and 'down'
platforms, it also maintained a public right of way but
despite its provision, the branch train was involved in
another accident on 13th September, 1892. Mr. William
Golding, a local greengrocer, was knocked over when
returning across the railway lines, having collected some
fish that was regularly left for him on the 'down' platform. The three Henley branch carriages were being
propelled into the station along the 'up' main line and
the whole train ran over him. He also died in Reading
hospital.

The construction work on the new goods yard that was
being built at Twyford was vastly overshadowed by the

quadrupling of the main line between Taplow and Didcot. The first section from Paddington to Taplow had been completed in 1884 but work on the remaining stretch was not begun until 1890. The additional running lines were built alongside the existing main line and passed through Twyford station behind the arrival platform. They were provided to ease the increasing congestion between Paddington and the junction at Didcot and were opened through Twyford for goods traffic in November, 1892, and for passenger traffic on 30th April the following year. Twyford station was rebuilt in connection with this work, new station buildings and a replacement footbridge being built by Messrs. S. & W. Pattinson while the new platforms, originally part of the same contract, were built by Messrs. A. Jackaman & Son.

At Shiplake, the original station building, believed to have been constructed of timber, was destroyed by fire on 26th August 1891, although rather curiously the matter was not reported in the local press. A temporary booking office and shelter was hastily erected in the entrance to the goods yard and plans for a new station were completed in November.

The new building prompted further improvements at the site which included an extension of the existing platform by a distance of 500 ft. in the 'up' direction. The platform surface beneath the canopy was paved with brick and the entire platform fenced off at the rear with timber palings. The extension necessitated the diversion of a public footpath which crossed at the end of the existing platform, to cross the line 500 ft. further south. A milk loading platform was constructed at the north end of the platform and nearby a new timber-built goods lock-up. A corrugated iron lamp hut was also provided at the south end of the station building, behind the platform fence.

In the goods yard a new siding was provided from a trailing connection in the 'down' direction from the short goods loop, the end of the siding being laid over the site of a pond which was filled in to provide the necessary land. A 3½ ton crane was also installed at this time and the yard surface alongside partially metalled. The estimated cost was £1,045, most of the work (£895) being carried out under contract by Mr. Alfred Simmonds, builder, of The Grove, Reading. The remainder, which for instance included the provision of the crane, was carried out by the GWR themselves.

Traders throughout the country had thought that the Railway and Canal Traffic Act, put into effect on 1st January 1893, would reduce goods rates, but instead they were increased. The ensuing outcry led to the Board of Trade authorizing the railways to apply rates equal to those operative on 31st December 1892 plus 5%. This came into force on 16th March 1893, so the public meeting about this held at Henley on 22nd March, was too late to be of any consequence.

The meeting was only attended by eleven people and two reporters from the local newspapers. It was claimed that the charges, which had increased by approximately 12% since the previous October, often exceeded the value of the goods themselves, and the rate for timber was so high between Reading and Henley that the merchants were using road transport. The possibility of bringing goods to Henley by river was investigated but the quantity would need to have been sufficient to load regularly one barge per week.

A constant source of frustration to the local traders at Henley was that the branch goods train, after arrival, was left throughout the morning on the opposite side of the running line to the goods yard. The branch goods left Reading each day at 5.00 a.m. and arrived at Henley at 6.30 a.m. It appears that the guard of this train then worked out with a passenger train from Henley so that the time spent at Henley on his initial arrival was short and consequently the wagons conveyed often did not get placed in the yard until about mid-day. The coal merchants were apparently in the habit of unloading the wagons where they stood, in order to save time, and carrying their goods over the running lines. This practice was, of course, entirely against regulations and frowned upon by the railway. Almost inevitably, an accident occurred on 4th January, 1894, when 27 year old William Leader, an

Another view of the new mill shortly after completion with the private siding in the foreground.
The Miller

employee of local coal merchant, Oliver Hopkins, was engaged in unloading a coal wagon with his brother. The accident occurred at about 8.00 a.m., at which time the 7.35 a.m. passenger train from Twyford to Henley, worked by the guard from the 5.00 a.m. goods, having first arrived at the terminus, was being propelled back out of the station as empty stock. William Leader was still unloading coal but, being rather deaf, did not hear the approaching stock and was knocked down and killed.

A proposal for a new railway at this time, a second route from London to Reading, was published in the *Henley and South Oxfordshire Standard* in January, 1894. The proposed railway, the London, High Wycombe, Great Marlow, Henley-on-Thames and Reading Railway, was to commence from a junction with the Midland Railway at Hendon and run a distance of some 40 miles through Harrow, Ruislip, Harefield, Chalfont St. Peter, Beaconsfield, Little Marlow, Great Marlow, Medmenham, Remenham, Henley-on-Thames, Harpsden, Shiplake, Caversham and terminate at Reading. The scheme was to include a four mile branch line from Beaconsfield through Loudwater to High Wycombe and another four mile branch from Chalfont St. Peter to Rickmansworth, terminating there by a junction with the London and North Western Railway.

The line was purely speculative as no survey had been made and the announcement was merely intended to sound out local support before any such steps were taken. It later became evident that this was only part of a very ambitious scheme as it was also intended to extend the line on from High Wycombe through Ibstone, Watlington, Dorchester, Abingdon, Bampton, Burford, Northleach and Charlton Kings to join the Midland Railway at Cheltenham. The line would then continue on through Ledbury, Leominster, and Bishops Castle to Newtown where it would join the Cambrian Railways, thus opening up a direct route from London to Mid-Wales and the Welsh coast. The suggested title for the scheme was the London, Cheltenham and Mid-Wales Direct Railway, but nothing more came of this.

Up to this time the GWR had simply referred to the line as the Henley branch, but in June 1894 they opened a new branch line to Henley-in-Arden, and from 1st January 1895 Henley officially became Henley-on-Thames.

A deputation from the townspeople of Henley visited the office of the Company Superintendent on 17th January, 1896, in the hope of securing improvements in the train service to Henley. In response the company looked into the matter and later sent the following letter to the Mayor dated 9th March, 1896.

Sir, referring to your visit at my office on 17th January last, together with Lord Camoys and other gentlemen forming a deputation from Henley on the question of the train service to and from Henley, I beg to say that various suggestions that

The earliest known view of a train on the branch. The loco appears to be a '517' class 0—4—2T crossing the viaduct on its way to Twyford, probably during the 1890s.
Courtesy C. B. Savory

A closer view of the ageing timbers of the Thames viaduct c.1895.   *British Railways*

were then made have received careful consideration and I am pleased to say that the directors have sanctioned the following alterations:—

1. The 8.45 a.m. train from Henley will be timed to arrive at Paddington at 9.45 a.m.
2. A new train will be timed to leave Henley at 9.35 a.m. arriving at Paddington at 10.37 a.m.
3. A new train will also be timed to leave Paddington at 10.50 a.m. arriving at Henley at 11.55 a.m. — the suggestion was that this train should start at 10.30, but it is not practical to time a train to leave Paddington at that time owing to important express trains leaving about that hour in the morning and 10.50 is the earliest time that can be adopted.
4. The 5.32 p.m. from Henley will be accelerated to reach Paddington at 6.50 p.m. — 20 minutes earlier than at present — and this is the utmost that can be done with that train.
5. We cannot run an independent train from Paddington to Henley about 9 o'clock, but a slip carriage will be attached to the 9.15 p.m. from Paddington timed to arrive at Henley about 10.20 p.m.

With regard to a late train being put on from Henley about 9.35 p.m. there will be a train during the summer months timed to leave Henley at 9.40 arriving at Paddington at 11 p.m. but we could not see our way to put on an entirely new train for Henley passengers. A suggestion was also made that cheap tickets should be issued from Henley to Paddington but this would be contrary to the usual practice adopted by this company, and I am sorry that we cannot see our way to carry out the suggestion. The service between Henley and the West of England, South Wales, &c shall be carefully looked into and if anything can be done to improve it you can accept my assurance that it shall not be overlooked.

The question of season ticket rates and arrangements shall also be considered and a further reply sent to you but I thought it well to give you an early advice of the alterations in the train services, which will be brought into operation on 1st May instead of 1st June as in previous years, and I hope this will be satisfactory to you and to the other gentlemen who formed the deputation.

We are considering a revision of the first and second class fares with regard to which a further communication shall be made to you.

It seems likely that their response was perhaps particularly favourable because at that time the GWR, in an attempt to revive second class traffic which had steadily decreased over a number of years, reduced fares from 1½d to 1¼d a mile. This had considerable success at first but following a subsequent decrease that later followed, second class travel was eliminated in 1910.

A subsequent letter from a Mr. Allen dated 7th May, 1896, read as follows:

Sir, — In further reference to my letter of 9th March, it has been decided in future to charge the following fares between Paddington and Henley.

First single 6/- instead of 6/3: second single 3/9 instead of 4/8: first return 10/6 instead of 10/9: second return 6/6 instead of 8/-.

The railway had greatly popularised Henley as a Thames-side resort, but the steadily increasing traffic had created considerable problems in operation, especially over the single line when 'up' and 'down' trains had to wait for each other. To improve the situation the terminus had already been expanded. In 1881 the main 'up' platform was extended and additional siding accommodation also provided for Mr. Wells, a local miller. He had to pay £100 towards the cost, an annual rent of £5, and 1/- for each of his trucks taken in or out of the siding. It is believed that the existing back siding was extended for his use and early in 1882 a 'roadway' was also constructed to provide access to the new siding. The board minutes also refer to a new siding which presumably replaced that removed to allow the platform extension.

In 1887 platform 2 was also lengthened and extensive new sidings were added either side of the running lines. The estimated cost for these improvements was £2,441 and the work was hastily completed in time for the regatta that year.

In 1895 some £495 was authorised for improving the gradient between Twyford and Shiplake, where filling was added to an embankment, and the following January it was once more decided to provide additional siding accommodation at Henley and extend the platforms even further, all of which was estimated at £3,770. New stables were also built to the west of the goods shed.

It is not clear whether on this occasion the work was completed in time for the regatta, as the Board of Trade inspection was not carried out until 31st August 1896. The excavation, ballasting, erection of platform walls, fencing, permanent way work, etc. was carried out by Messrs. Jackaman & Son (estimated cost £1,563) while the remainder was carried out by GWR men with materials from the company's stores.

The revised layout incorporated a double line out of the station as far as Mill Lane Crossing, the laying in of new and alteration of existing connections, resignalling and the construction of two new signal boxes. The replacement station box, of blue engineering brick, was built alongside its smaller predecessor and housed a 65-lever frame. The one at Mill Lane was similar in style but much smaller, having only a 13-lever frame and a gate wheel to control the level crossing. According to the plans the crossing had been re-equipped with larger gates to accommodate double track although the arrangement was short lived.

Despite the improvements carried out on each occasion, the limitations of the single line were severe for the exceptional regatta traffic, and inevitably the Great Western finally decided that the time had arrived to double the line. The estimated cost of the work was £21,275 and the recommendation of the Traffic Committee to double the line was adopted at a Board Meeting held on 23rd July, 1896.

The contract for the doubling was awarded to Mr. George Palmer, and the company ordered the work to be completed in time for the regatta the following year.

As already mentioned, the line had been built to allow for the provision of double track and, although to minimise the cost of construction at the time, some of the earth works were only completed for single track, the over-bridges were built for double track, and the single running line laid to one side of the formation to allow for a possible 'down' line alongside.

Mr. George Palmer's contract commenced from the 31¼ mile post at Twyford, up to and including the point at Henley where the line crossed Mill Lane, and included earthworks, fencing, laying ballast and permanent way, widening viaducts, etc. and alterations to Shiplake station (estimated cost £8,000). The Thames viaduct was put out under a separate contract and the remainder of the work was to be carried out by the company.

The timber span of one of the original overbridges carrying Wargrave Lane over the railway had already been replaced with wrought iron plate girders in 1894 and the plans for an entirely new overbridge just outside Twyford, at 31 miles 40 chains, had been drawn up in May. The GWR granted the right to construct the bridge over the railway to builder F. Walters Bond, Esq., the vendor of 187 acres of land known as the Loddon Park Estate, who undertook to complete the bridge over the railway within six months of the date of the sale. The land concerned was part of the Wargrave Manor Estate and was divided by the course of the Henley branch. The land on the west side of the railway was served by a new approach road which at the time crossed the line by means of a level crossing. The land was auctioned in August, 1896, and two years later the 1898 *Guide and Directory to Twyford* said 'The sale of building plots in Wargrave Road together with the erection of the substantial bridge over the Henley branch railway making the land on the west side of the line also available has given an incentive to the erection of villas which will not only improve the appearance of the neighbourhood but will bring a class of residents who will be helpful to local trade.'

In the event, only the land along the east of the line was developed and the 'estate road' that had been known as Goffe's Lane remained unmetalled.

This new bridge was to have been in lieu of two accommodation crossings further 'down' the line, but the further of the pair, which had previously been the sole means of access to Twyfordfield Farm, at approximately 32 miles 5 chains, in fact continued in use as a farm crossing.

The doubling of the line entailed the excavation and banking of earthworks through much of the route, mainly on the 'down' side, the total excavation being some 22,437 cubic yards, whilst the banking totalled 21,641 cubic yards. The culverts all needed extending, having only been constructed for single track. The flood arch at 33 miles 1 chain, a simple timber structure, was replaced with a substantial three span blue brick arched viaduct which later became known as Wargrave Viaduct. The floodstream that it crossed was diverted to pass beneath the structure at right angles to the line. The viaduct over the Thames, which had come to be known as Shiplake Viaduct, as already mentioned, was a separate contract, and although the doubling was undertaken because of the increasing traffic, the possibility does exist that the condition of the ageing Thames and Lashbrook timber viaducts may have contributed to the company's decision, although it must be said that this is pure conjecture.

The estimated cost of reconstruction of Shiplake Viaduct was £13,500 and tenders for the work were invited in January 1896 for building piers and abutments with materials supplied by the GWR, for the supply and erection of ironwork for the centre spans and for the erection of second-hand girders and flooring apparently recovered from viaducts which had been rebuilt in South Devon.

Looking downstream to the old viaduct.   *Courtesy Miss S. Reeves*

This pre-1916 view shows the modified station at Shiplake, looking towards Henley. The original line is shown on the right.

Author's collection

To aid the construction work, a temporary siding trailing from the 'down' direction was installed on the embankment on the Shiplake side of the viaduct near the 33¼ mile post. With the capacity to hold six wagons and an engine, it was controlled by a two-lever ground frame and approved by the Board of Trade on 3rd August 1896.

Later a temporary connection to the new 'down' line was also installed on the other side of the river by the 33 mile post. This was controlled from a new 13 lever (6 in use) signal box situated on the 'up' side of the embankment between the flood arch and the viaduct. The new box was also an electric train staff block post and was brought into use on 1st February 1897.

Lashbrook Viaduct was also replaced, as part of the main contract, with a plate girder structure, similar in appearance to the Thames Viaduct, of which the first of the six steel girder spans bridged a farm accommodation crossing. During the doubling it was found necessary to place one of the telegraph poles on land belonging to a Mrs. Blackburn at Shiplake. In return she was granted access to the river by right of way along the stream under Lashbrook Viaduct, each party to the agreement paying 5/- per annum for the privilege.

Substantial modification was necessary to make the recently rebuilt station at Shiplake suitable for double track. The new running line diverged from the end of Lashbrook Viaduct and was routed behind the existing station building and platform, converging again alongside the goods yard. The platform was converted to an island platform between the two running lines and at the same time extended a distance of 100 ft to the south involving a further diversion of the public footpath. The new

station building was retained and converted to an island platform building by extending the canopy all the way round the structure.

A station master's house, new signal box and footbridge were also provided, the latter spanning the total width of the site to provide passenger access to the platform. It was also a means of crossing the line other than the level crossing, which thereafter passengers were not officially allowed to use.

The provisional plans submitted to the Board of Trade still showed only a simple occupation crossing for the lane leading to the river. The Board of Trade did not favour this and recommended that the gates should be controlled from the signal box. The GWR agreed and a standard level crossing was installed. The new layout also involved rearranging the goods yard which included the repositioning of the recently installed yard crane and the provision of a new siding.

Between Shiplake and Henley the remaining culverts were extended and the recently re-equipped level crossing at Mill Lane, just outside Henley, was replaced with a new overbridge which was again constructed of blue engineering brick with steel plate girder spans. This bridge was constructed immediately north of the existing level crossing and Mill Lane was diverted to run over it after obtaining the necessary Parliamentary consent.

At Henley the alterations were minimal. The new 'down' running line was connected to the end of the recently extended loop, and nearby on the north side of the level crossing a catchpoint protected the station. The pointwork at the foot of the bay platform was also modified, together with some of the pointwork on the station approach. The turntable was bolted from a new four-lever ground frame, which also worked a catchpoint and disc, this frame in turn being bolted from the signal box.

The extensive carriage sidings, which reached as far as Mill Lane level crossing, had to be shortened by a few feet to allow for the approaches of the new overbridge. Two of the sidings, one each side of the running line, were in fact extended with temporary track which curved sharply through 90° east and west respectively alongside the approaches to facilitate the delivery of infill during construction.

Finally, much, if not the whole, of the branch was also refenced with post and wire fencing. Incidentally, it was following meetings of the Locomotive, Carriage & Stores and Engineering Committees respectively during 1891 that it was decided to bring 'iron wire' fencing (in lieu of wooden fencing) more generally into use on the GWR as the opportunity arose, wooden fencing thereafter only being used in exceptional circumstances.

In October 1896, in the midst of this work, the Wargrave Parish Council resolved, against the wishes of their chairman, to ask the GWR to reconsider the question of opening a station at Wargrave. They had applied the previous April. Whilst the company eventually agreed to this, they concentrated their efforts on completing the work in hand to meet their own rapidly approaching deadline.

No incidents were reported in the local press in connection with the doubling of the line but on Christmas Eve one young man had a lucky escape from an accident that occurred at Twyford Mill. A coal train was being shunted on to the branch at Twyford when, on rounding the curve by the goods shed, one of the couplings broke and 13 wagons and a brake van ran away down the steep gradient and into the private mill siding. The guard applied his brake and jumped clear from the van. There were several wagons standing in the mill premises but fortunately a young man unloading one of them at the time realised what was happening and managed to get clear before the runaway vehicles smashed the wagon in which he was standing and drove the other wagons off the rails, breaking down a large timber and earth buffer stop. A telegraph pole apparently prevented one or more wagons from plunging into the river.

At the beginning of June 1897 the GWR announced in the local paper that serious drawbacks had resulted from the floods that winter and that this had considerably hindered the work of doubling. The contractors regretted that they would not be able to open the double line for the regatta as hoped. A month later, however, after an all out effort, the work was sufficiently advanced to allow the Board of Trade inspection to be carried out by Colonel York, R.E., on 12th July, just two days before the regatta, the GWR stating that they were 'most anxious to have the

An earlier postcard view with the fireman of No. 463 looking out for the right of way before departing for Henley. *Courtesy Reg Daniells*

benefit of the new line of rails for the additional traffic over the branch'. The new gradients of the running line between Twyford and Shiplake did not correspond with the old line as the opportunity had been taken to improve them. Also whilst the new line was carried over the three new viaducts, the old timber ones remained undisturbed beneath the old line for the time being.

Following the inspection the company obtained permission to bring the new line into use for passenger traffic and the company proudly announced that it would after all be ready just in time for the regatta that July.

The *Railway Magazine* reported that the railway traffic to the regatta that year had beaten all previous records,

which must have been a great comfort to the GWR after all their efforts and expenditure. The same journal also said that the special 'down' trains in the morning and 'up' trains at night ran at intervals of only a few minutes, many of them performing the journey without an intermediate stop.

After the regatta it was necessary to revert to single line operation between Twyford and Shiplake, the new line being utilized until the original viaducts had been replaced and the gradients brought into line with the new works. The single line arrangements started on Sunday, 25th July, a properly interlocked crossover being provided just north of Shiplake level crossing where double track

Two views of the replacement Thames viaduct just prior to completion.   *British Railways*

recommenced. At the end of Lashbrook Viaduct the new 'down' line was temporarily slewed to connect with the original line through the station and a temporary 'down' starting signal was placed opposite the platform just short of the level crossing.

The doubling was finally completed by 11th July 1898 and inspected on 24th October. The inspecting officer placed a weight restriction on the ageing Bolney bridge but was moved to remark that the new viaducts and culverts were of 'excellent workmanship'. The temporary signal box near the Thames viaduct was in the event retained for use as a block post controlling home and distant signals in each direction. It was used 'for busy days such as those of the Henley Regatta'.

In addition to £7,283. 0s. 7d. paid to George Palmer for the main contract, a further payment of approximately £900 is recorded for certain works originally intended to be carried out by the company's own men, namely sidings at Shiplake, alterations to the gradient, planting hedges, etc. Palmer also received a further payment of £1,475 for gradient improvements (authorised in July 1897) this time on the old line, each side of Shiplake Viaduct.

While the doubling of the branch was still undergoing completion, the GWR prepared plans for a scheme to extend the branch from Henley to Marlow. This was one of a number of schemes on various parts of the Great Western for which it had been decided at a board meeting on 23rd July to instigate the preparation of plans in order that the company might consider the promotion of a Bill in the ensuing session of Parliament.

In the event, the Bill put forward did include the Henley to Marlow Railway. Briefly, the proposals for this entailed doubling the company's existing branch line to Marlow, together with the southern part of the Wycombe line from Bourne End to Maidenhead, and extending the Henley branch a distance of some nine miles along the valley of the River Thames to connect with the Marlow branch, thus enabling through trains to run from High Wycombe and Paddington to Henley via Marlow.

The proposals were immediately announced in the press and the *Henley Standard* of 3rd December, 1897, reported that the Council were 'only too glad to welcome anything that would give an impetus to the influx of visitors' and that a small committee had already been appointed to watch the proposal and ensure that the interests of the town were protected.

The new line was to leave the existing Henley branch at a point between Sheephouse Farm and Mill Lane and run towards the Thames on a rising embankment, crossing the river by means of a two arched bridge, the centre support of which was to rest on one of the eyots. On the opposite bank the line was to continue on a high embankment through Thamesfield, which was the chosen site of the new station, and across the Oxford to London road by means of a viaduct. This would have been situated near the junction between this road and Remenham Lane, not far in fact from the famous Leander Rowing Club House. From here the line was to continue along the river to Marlow. The existing Henley station was to have been retained for goods traffic only.

The proposed route was vigorously opposed by the local people who naturally feared that it would ruin the beautiful riverside for which Henley was acclaimed. They were naturally also reluctant to accept the idea of the station being removed to the opposite side of the river.

Sir J. E. Edwards-Moss, who resided at Thamesfield (the site of the proposed station), was one of the first to protest in a letter that was published in *The Field* and was also reproduced in the *Henley Standard* of 3rd December. The letter was most critical of the scheme and concluded by saying:

> I believe that those who have rowed and won honour, if not also medals or cups, at Henley, have a deep affection for the scene of their labours — an affection which time does not impair — and would be seriously grieved to see its scenery marred by the hideous eyesore which the Great Western Railway are seeking Parliamentary powers to erect. I cannot but think that the announcement of it will be received with horror by oarsmen all over the world. And I hope that English rowing clubs may be found willing to make strong and active protest against a Bill which proposes thus to deface and desecrate a spot held by most of us oarsmen, whether of the present or the past, in no little veneration.

The *Henley Standard* for the following week, under the heading of 'Henley's Great Peril' reproduced a letter that had appeared in the *Pall Mall Gazette*.

> Sir, — I notice in your issue of 25th ult., under the heading, that Mr. Wilkinson, General Manager of the Great Western Railway, stated to your representatives that 'The Great Western Railway is as much interested as anybody in preserving the natural beauties of the district through which its system passes'. It has not done much at present to preserve the natural beauties of the Thames by building that hideous viaduct at Windsor, the most unsightly embankment running parallel with the water at Tilehurst, and the two dreadful iron bridges lately erected at Bourne End and Shiplake. If these and other eyesores put up by the Great Western Railway are Mr. Wilkinson's idea of improving the natural beauty of the Thames scenery, we shall know what to expect in the proposed ornamental bridge across the river at Henley. No wonder there is so much outcry raised by all lovers of the river scenery against future schemes proposed by the Great Western Railway.

> I am, yours faithfully, N.P.

The following extract from *The Lady* was also reproduced in the same issue:

> What would the round of our summer pleasures be without Henley? For a vulgarised Henley, with the shriek of the railway engine on the bank of the river, and the straight walls of a railway station defacing the landscape would no longer be the place we love for the beauty of its surroundings, as well as for the sport we enjoy there. While railways are necessary evils and, even if we could, we would scarcely do away with them, let us at least do what in us lies to preserve our choicest haunts of nature from their profanation.

A public meeting to consider the proposals was held on 11th February, 1898, in the Town Hall at Henley. The townspeople were unanimous in their opposition to the scheme outlined in the Bill as it was felt that the railway would seriously detract from the superb scenery which, as Councillor Simmons put it, was the town's 'stock in trade'.

The GWR sent revised plans along to this meeting showing a tunnel through White Hill which it was hoped

The 1898 Henley Regatta staff officials grouped on the edge of what appears to be the original turntable. They are *(from left to right, standing)* R. May, Cab Inspector, Reading; A. Poultney, Platform Inspector, Plymouth; E. Jones, Lamp Inspector, Paddington; A. Allen, Platform Inspector, Reading; G. G. Ackland, District Inspector, Didcot; F. Smith, Cab Inspector, Oxford; *(seated)* F. Pearce, Chief Ticket Inspector, Hereford; J. Short, Relief Clerk, Reading, W. Thomas, District Inspector, Reading; J. Lock, Station-master, Henley-on-Thames; E. H. Hunt, Relief Clerk, Reading; H. Griffin, Platform Inspector, Didcot.

GWR Magazine

would overcome the local objections. However, the new station was then to be located on the site of the allotment grounds that were situated a short distance up White Hill. This greatly displeased the townspeople as the station was still to be located on the opposite side of the river. Quite apart from the obvious inconvenience it was felt that 'it would be an immense injury to the town if the thousands of persons coming by train were deposited on the opposite side of the town and close to the regatta course.' Whilst the GWR had said that they would continue to run excursion trains to the old station, there was no guarantee as to how long this arrangement would continue, and it 'seemed preposterous' to them not to have a station at Henley as it would cease to be Henley station if it were situated out of the borough as well as the County.

It appears that at this stage local people were quite unaware of the scheme in full as it was not until a subsequent meeting held on 18th February that the Mayor reported that the GWR did not wish to connect Henley with Marlow alone, 'because if they did he should think that they were the most unwise people on the face of the earth . . . . But this scheme of theirs is a part of a much larger scheme which is to connect the direct line through High Wycombe to London and to fill up the gap between Henley and Marlow. They framed the most barbarous plan that could be prepared by any railway company in the Kingdom . . . . and he believed that the Great Western Company felt so themselves at the present moment.'

He also reported that at a meeting with the GWR's engineer he had been assured that because of the engineering difficulties it was impossible to build a station on the Henley side of the river.

One of the councillors said that he did not think it would be possible to carry a proposal against a new railway to Henley as 'they were face to face with a proposal of one of the finest companies to extend their railway, and what they were called upon to do is to take care that the proposals are so carried out as to produce the best possible effects upon the town.'

The Great Western were certainly anxious to overcome the opposition from the town as the tunnel alone would

apparently have cost some £50,000 and yet the company conceded still further by revising their scheme yet again in order that the new station could be located on the Oxfordshire side of the river as requested.

The town's success in achieving such a concession was proudly announced at a meeting held in the town hall at Henley on Wednesday, 2nd March, and was justifiably regarded as a triumph. In the final scheme the new railway was to have begun to the south of Sheephouse Farm, and run to the west of the same, across Mill Lane, passing close to the steam laundry, before reaching the site of the proposed station. This would have been situated in the field behind Canadian Terrace, about a quarter of a mile further south than the existing one. A new road was to have been built from the vicinity of what has since become the Three Horseshoes public house, and run diagonally across the field to serve the station. The line would then have crossed the river, then over the Wargrave Road (not far from Thamesfield) and run across the Binns before entering a tunnel through Remenham Hill.

The Thames Conservancy Commissioners and the boating interest had meanwhile raised fierce opposition and, led by Sir Frederick Dixon-Hartland, M.P., lodged a petition at the Private Bill Office at the House of Commons opposing the new works Bill of the GWR. Their obstructive attitude had previously been severely criticised in *Herepath's Railway Journal* of February 11th. 'All this in special pleading in the interest of those who do not want their boat houses disturbed'.

In the face of this opposition, despite the GWR having arrived at a compromise that was agreeable between themselves and the town, the company deferred their application to Parliament and the General Manager sent a letter to the Mayor of Henley outlining the situation and concluding:

On March 18th the Company were led to expect that their intentions would be received with satisfaction and approbation, and particularly so when they had, at the insistence of those who were entitled to speak for the town of Henley and for the district, endeavoured to remove all difficulties by contemplating an expense which practically meant double the cost of the railway that was originally surveyed. It is, however, understood that strongly-held objections still prevail, and the Company are reluctantly compelled to the conclusion that more time is needed to enable their intentions to be better understood and that it will be the better course to defer for a time their application to Parliament.

It is thought right to make this the intimation without waiting until the Bill reaches a further stage, in order that those who do not agree as to the advantages of the proposal may not be placed under the necessity of incurring the expense of further proceedings in opposing them.

Thanking you for the courtesy and perfect fairness which you have invariably displayed in the course of the negotiations, I am, dear Mr. Mayor your faithful servant.
(Signed) J. L. Wilkinson.

After all their opposition and concern it seems that the local people regretted the abandonment of the Henley and Marlow Railway and the Mayor replied to the GWR expressing the Council's regret and expressing the hope that the railway might be brought forward again in the future — but this was not to be.

Traffic on the branch continued to flourish and the 1898 regatta was particularly notable as reported in the following extract from the *Great Western Railway Magazine* that year.

The 1898 Henley Regatta will long be remembered by the officials who took part in it, on account of its dissimilarities from previous years. The traffic on the first day was 2,556 decrease on 1897, and the second day 932 decrease, and everybody looked forward to a great falling off, but on the third day there was an increase of 3,393 or a total of 37,513 for the three days. The Regatta can clearly be called a record from every point of view, the weather was the very best that could be desired, not even the inevitable shower to remind old friends that it was Henley week, whereas the working was almost perfection, the whole of the outward-booked trains

leaving to time, although several were run in duplicate, and not one incoming train arrived during the three days but what was run without obstruction to the platforms. The working reflects the greatest credit on the arrangements made and to the officials who carried them out. The whole working was under the personal direction of Mr. Gibbs, the Divisional Supt.

The *Railway Magazine* also reported that 'despite the ample reserve of carriages, for which the Great Western is noted, almost every other railway entering London lent trains to the Great Western to help to convey the crowds to Henley this year.'

During May the following year, the heavy traffic being dealt with by the railway was reflected in a complaint made by local traders expressing their anxiety over the provision of long promised improvements in the goods department, where apparently the lack of accommodation for goods was a frequent annoyance. The outcome was the lengthening of the 'back siding' in 1904. This was slewed, extended and reconnected to one of the carriage sidings which was then used as a headshunt. The work may have been partly financed by Toomer's who paid £285 for siding accommodation at Henley that year.

In July 1899 the GWR invited tenders for the construction of a new station at Wargrave. Why this village had not origianlly been provided with a station is not clear. A drawing of a wooden station building for Seend and Semington, dated 1857, was also designated for use at Wargrave but never built, although this could have been the building for Shiplake. Despite the fact that the line passed so close to the village of Wargrave, it was not until this time, and after further prompting from the villagers, that the long awaited station was actually provided.

The provisional site plan incorporated an existing occupation crossing at the north end of the platforms, but it seems that despite proposed modifications to the

The new station at Wargrave.   *Courtesy Chris Hopes*

The view south from the signal box in 1902. The approaching train, hauled by a 'Metro' class 2—4—0T, is signalled for the 'arrival' platform, No. 2.

G. W. Reeves, courtesy Miss S. Reeves

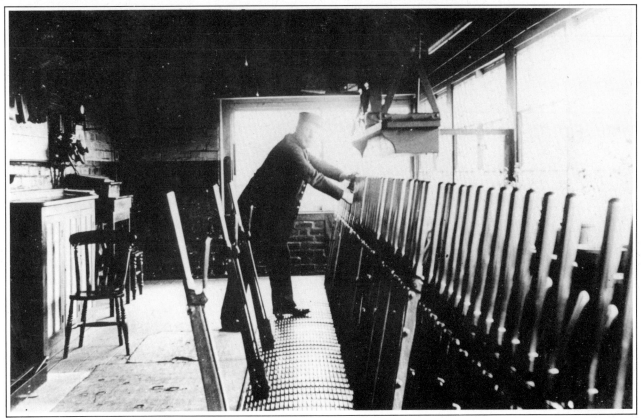

A contemporary photograph of the interior of Henley Signal Box.

G. W. Reeves, courtesy Miss S. Reeves

approaches, it was not retained. The necessary land was purchased in the same year and a new approach road built from the village to the station site. The station was constructed to a typical and standard Great Western design of the period with a traditional track layout and two platforms connected by a covered footbridge, as shown on page 31. The main station building was situated on the 'up' platform and supplemented with a corrugated iron lock-up. A small waiting room only was provided on the 'down' side and a corrugated iron lamp shed together with a new signal box were situated at the south end of the platform.

Again the erection of the station buildings, footbridge and platform walls was put out to contract (estimate £2,500) the remaining work being completed by the company, the total cost being estimated at £4,690. The station was gas lit from the outset, the work again being carried out by the contractor for an additional £100.

Although the Board of Trade inspection was not carried out until 6th December, the new station opened on Monday, 1st October, 1900. It had even been used prior to completion on the occasion of the Wargrave Regatta on Saturday, 18th August, when several of the afternoon 'down' trains stopped to drop off visitors, who were left to make their own way back to Twyford station. It is believed that the signal box was not opened until 2nd January, 1901, although this has not been confirmed. However, it seems likely that this new 19 lever box (15 in use and 4 spare) simultaneously replaced the temporary

box near the river. The station house was not provided until 1902.

The last 'down' train in the evening which served Wargrave was at 7.22 p.m. and the local residents not surprisingly expressed their concern that some passengers would still have to walk from Twyford which had been their local station prior to this.

During the year 1900 the GWR amended the train services, commencing on 1st May, and brought Henley within 50 minutes of Paddington, with new direct expresses with no intermediate stops, leaving Paddington for Henley at 10.00 a.m., and Henley for Westbourne Park and Paddington at 9.15 p.m. The previous 10.40 a.m. from Henley was replaced with a new through fast train leaving Henley at 11.10 a.m. and another through train at 6.20 p.m., each reaching Paddington an hour later. The 9.05 a.m. from Paddington connected at Twyford for Henley enabling passengers to arrive at 10.05 a.m. The 12.05 p.m. from Paddington to Windsor ran forward from Slough to Henley direct, arriving at 1.05 p.m., and a new fast train left Paddington at 2.15 p.m. arriving at Henley at 3.15 p.m. On Sunday new direct expresses were also introduced to leave Paddington at 10.05 a.m. and Henley at 9.00 p.m. and other services were also improved.

In the same year the inaugural trip of a combined rail and river excursion from Paddington took place on Tuesday, 29th May. The tickets were 21/- and included a first class railway journey to and from Henley, a trip on the river by steam launch with luncheon served on board, and

Another view from the signal box, this time looking over the station. It was actually taken on the same occasion and immediately after the arrival of the train shown on page 32. The departing train, hauled by another 'Metro' class tank, is the local branch train for Twyford. The aperture just visible through the opposite end of the roof led out to the original turntable and the congested back siding was still connected in front of the signal box at this time.

G. W. Reeves, courtesy Miss S. Reeves

dinner at the Red Lion Hotel, before returning to the station. The excursion was tried for four days a week during June and was so well patronised that it was run daily from 1st July.

The provision of a new turntable at Henley in 1903 marked the beginning of what were to be the last major changes at the station. The new 55 ft turntable, of the modern balanced type, was installed in the loco yard alongside the station. This came so close to the north-western boundary and the public footpath, known as Cold Bath footpath, that skirted the same, that Parliamentary authorisation had to be obtained to divert about 11 chains of the path eastwards in order to clear the new works.

The old 45 ft. turntable, which incidentally was decked all over with timber planking, was removed in February the following year. The running line was terminated under the roof and a new engine release crossover was provided alongside platform No. 1. This work brought about the provision of a new broad carriageway over the site of the old turntable straight across the station entrance towards the river, and the northern end of the overall roof was enclosed with an entirely new booking hall. Prior to this, entry to the platforms had been made through a double entrance in the side of the station building and passengers had left through a double exit in the northern end of the station. The new booking hall, housing a semi-circular office enclosed with timber panelling, obviously relieved the congested station building, the rooms of the former booking office providing a more spacious parcels office from which parcels could be loaded direct into horse-drawn vans that could be driven up to what was the

This snapshot of two local gentlemen, Harry Ive and Ted Pullens, provides a glimpse of Toomers' original coal office. The replacement building is featured below.

G. W. Reeves, courtesy Miss S. Reeves

The newly completed entrance hall enclosing the north end of the overall roof. The broad carriageway was built over the site of the old turntable.
Lens of Sutton

The station frontage c.1905.   *Author's collection*

entrance. The old parcels office was converted into a bicycle room. The main building had already been enlarged by a southwards extension in 1891. This was carefully matched to the design of the original and provided increased W.C. and urinal accomodation, the former urinals being converted into a cloakroom. The station had incidentally been repainted in 1901.

The bookstall, which at the time was leased by Messrs. W. H. Smith, was replaced with a new structure that was

One of the parcels delivery vehicles built in 1900. *British Railways*

erected beyond the buffer stops at the end of platform No. 1. The small parcels weighing machine was moved away from the buffer stops and located alongside the wall enclosing the rear of the new ticket office.

Passenger shelter was also increased by the provision of a new platform canopy that extended to the south from the overall roof, along the main platform. A house was built on the company's property, in the meadow to the west of the station, for the station master, Mr. Lock.

The new improvements were additionally welcome because of the high number of unemployed in the town at that time, a large number of whom were employed on work connected with the improvements. The contractors were Messrs. C. H. Hunt who successfully undertook to complete the work by the 18th June. The remaining modifications were completed in October and inspected by the Board of Trade on 15th November.

Messrs. Toomer R. & Co., local coal merchants, had occupied a small ivy clad office adjacent to the original turntable, but this building was swept away during the improvements. During this work the company operated from a temporary office in Imperial Parade, opposite the station, while the G.W.R. constructed a substantial replacement brick office for them to the east of the station, alongside the new roadway.

It seems likely that it was at this time that the fence enclosing the station forecourt was removed. This may have dated from about 1877 when the local council took over Station Road. Its removal left the forecourt open again and another fence was erected further south to enclose the goods yard. Following these improvements, the station had taken on the overall appearance that it was to keep for the next 60 years or so.

CHAPTER FOUR

THE GLORY FADES

1904-47

THE Henley Branch was close to the Great Western Signalling Department headquarters at Reading, and, having been recently doubled, was therefore the obvious choice and ideal testing ground for experiments that were carried out with automatic train control apparatus which gave audible signals to the driver when approaching distant signals.

The system was entirely worked out by the company's staff and patents for the GWR audible warning system were granted in the first instance to Messrs. Jacobs, Insell, Newton and Bowden and in the second instance to Messrs. Jacobs and Insell, all GWR staff members. The system was developed at Reading under the direction of Mr. A. T. Blackall, the company's engineer, and experiments began on the Henley branch at the end of 1905. Briefly, the apparatus involved consisted of an inverted T-bar mounted on a 40 ft. baulk of timber that was laid longitudinally between the rails. The branch locomotives were fitted with a sprung contact shoe which projected beneath and was raised 1½ inches in height when passing over the ramp. The ramps preceded each distant signal and were electrified when the signal was off, the current passing through the shoe ringing a bell in the cab. Conversely, when the signal was on, or the apparatus had failed, the ramp was electrically dead and the raising of the shoe broke a local circuit on the engine, thereby causing a steam whistle to blow in the cab until cancelled by the driver.

This system proved so reliable that on 1st December, 1906, a more extended trial commenced on the Fairford branch, a single line of some 22 miles, on which the distant signals were replaced entirely with warning ramps and on which only engines equipped with the apparatus were permitted.

In November, 1908, ramps were installed at all distant signals on the quadruple track main line between Reading and Slough, and later, by 1910, to Paddington. The audible

A branch train from Twyford about to pass over an ATC ramp by Mill Lane signal box c.1914. *Courtesy John Crocker*

system was changed to automatic train control by making the same operation that worked the audible warning additionally open a valve that admitted air, thus destroying the vacuum which held the brakes off, and subsequently stopping the train. This system came to be used all over the GWR and made a considerable contribution towards some of the principles employed in the magnetic induction system subsequently introduced and finally standardised by British Railways.

The branch was in the news again in 1914 when on 4th May a new railmotor service to Henley commenced. The new service ran from Reading to Basingstoke at 12.15 p.m. and 5.55 p.m., from Reading to Twyford and Henley at 10.56 a.m., 2.20 p.m. and 3.43 p.m., and from Henley to Reading at 11.43 a.m., 2.58 p.m., and 5.08 p.m., making convenient connections at Reading with various services.

A railmotor service between Henley and Windsor had first been proposed as early as 1904, but the 1914 timetable marked the commencement of a service from Reading that was destined to survive the G.W.R.

With the outbreak of the Great War in 1914, the Government took over all the railways in the country which effectively meant that government traffic had precedence and was carried without charge, and that the receipts of all of the companies were pooled and divided in proportion to the net receipts of each during the year.

The GWR immediately announced the suspension of all cheap tickets except workmen's, but the issue of these recommenced on Monday, 17th August, followed by the re-issue of excursion tickets on Thursday, 20th August. Cheap bookings, however, only continued until 29th March, 1915, and tourist tickets only until 1st May, 1916.

The station lighting at Henley was greatly reduced and consequently the platform edges had been whitewashed by 1916. In a letter to the local newspaper in January that year, the station master appealed to local people to keep all blinds drawn and in the poor visibility to refrain from alighting from trains before they had stopped, in the hope of reducing the risk of casualties, and pointed out that little time was saved in doing otherwise.

With minimal cutbacks the ordinary service was fully maintained but railways generally were decidedly stretched with nearly a third of the Great Western's employees enlisted in the forces and special wartime traffic to cope with. However, it seems that the Henley branch was little affected and it was as late as March 1917 that the company announced a curtailment in road delivery services and a restriction in the delivery area. Wagons were in short supply throughout the country and a penal increase in demurrage charges was enforced to help to reduce the time wasted by wagons standing in sidings.

As far as has been ascertained, during the economic depression following the First World War, the signal box at Mill Lane, Henley, was closed after the 1919 regatta. For some years prior to this the box had been out of use other than during the period of the regatta, at which time

An Edwardian summer's day outside Henley station.

British Railways

An undated view of open cab 'Metro' No. 976 awaiting departure from platform No. 1. This winter scene with the Thames in flood shows the riverside before the 1920s development.
W. L. Kenning, courtesy Adrian Vaughan

it had been switched in to provide another block section to cope with the intensive service, and manned by a relief signalman from Reading.

The two signals are said to have remained for some ten years or so afterwards but with 'out of use' crosses affixed to their arms.

Railwaymen at Henley, in common with the rest of the country, came out on strike for an increase in pay and better working conditions, on Saturday morning, 27th

September, 1919, after which no trains ran to or from Henley. The strike was sudden and came as a great surprise to the majority of local people who were unaware of any such trouble. Only the station master and booking clerks were on duty at the station and one of the clerks took the mail into Twyford.

The milk churns were collected on Sunday and taken to London by motor transport. This continued throughout the strike and processions of lorries were reported going

A group of young volunteers for the army pose for the photographer on 5th August 1914 just before taking the train to Oxford.

Courtesy E. Leaver

The former crossing keeper's cottage at Mill Lane. The design of this building was similar to that used at the stations on the Wycombe Railway. The gentleman in shirtsleeves is Ernest Paice, a signalman at Henley for 21 years. He died in 1917 aged 45.   *Courtesy Mrs. Cutbush*

through the town laden with milk or returning with empty churns. Even a clergyman was seen driving a four ton lorry laden with milk to London. Pickets had been sent to urge the men to strike but their efforts were in vain.

Local people were asked to use wood blocks instead of coal wherever possible and the pressure of gas was reduced during the night in an effort to conserve coal supplies.

The Mayor of Henley sent a telegram to Paddington offering volunteer assistance, in response to which a service of seven trains each way on the branch was arranged for Friday, 3rd October. However, the strike was settled on 5th October.

Volunteers are believed to have played a more active part during the General Strike a few years later. It commenced at midnight on Monday, 3rd May, 1926, lasting through until the 14th. There were no trains on the branch until, it is thought, the Wednesday afternoon, when apparently a '63XX' class 2—6—0 brought a goods train to Henley. The locomotive was manned by some four or five volunteers amongst whom was a clergyman.

A shedman known as 'Captain Cook' drove the branch engine over the line during the second week of the strike together with Billy Brain, a local taxi driver who acted as fireman.

At the end of 1923 an engine arriving at Henley station one evening was involved in a collision. The accident occurred in thick fog on Sunday, 9th December, when 'County' class tank No. 2244 was running light engine into the station and, unable to stop at the home signal, collided with the end of the train that was stabled in platform No. 2. The leading vehicle, clerestory third No. 1890, sustained considerable damage but there was little damage to the engine. At this time the coaches were left all day in

this platform on Sundays until a light engine collected them for the 6.20 p.m. service.

Another incident involving a 'County' class tank occurred on 18th November, 1925, when No. 2250 was involved in a collision at Henley station. No. 2250, having run bunker first over the release crossover from platform No. 1, collided with the Henley branch loco, 'Metro' class

Bert Broad as a young lad porter at Shiplake c.1920.
Courtesy Gary Broad

Wargrave station, looking towards Henley in 1919.

L & GRP courtesy David & Charles

2—4—0T No. 469, which was coming off the shed at the same time. No. 469 sustained severe damage to the front buffer, leading axle box, smoke box and lower part of the water tank, while the rear steps of No. 2250 were slightly damaged. 'Duke' class 4—4—0 *Cornubia* worked the branch service until Thursday morning.

The first time that a 'Castle' class locomotive was turned at Henley, about 1926-7, proved to be a memorable occasion for all concerned. The locomotive, No. 4032 *Queen Alexandra*, was in fact a rebuilt 'Star' class 4—6—0, and therefore presumed to fit on to the turntable, as with other locomotives of this class. No. 4032 had worked the 6.15 p.m. from Paddington into Henley, put the stock away into the sidings and was being turned in readiness to work out again with the 7.30 p.m. to Reading. In the event, the overall wheelbase of the loco and tender was

Henley station in 1919.

L & GRP courtesy David & Charles

The Henley station staff 1925. They are from left to right: Teddy Clemson, porter; Arthur Tristem; 3 unknown; Bob Lawrence, goods porter; Jim Spearing, Frank Taylor, signalman; Bert Smith, guard; Jimmy Jones, carman; *seated:* A. Kitley, guard; unknown; Joseph Lock, station master; unknown; Bill Rixon, shunter; *Front row:* Reg Ayres, porter unknown; - Eustace; unknown.

Courtesy J. Jones

Ernest Paice, signalman, holding his 4½ year old son, outside the crossing keeper's cottage at Mill Lane. On the right are his father, his wife and 1½ year old daughter. The dog's name was Toby. Mr. Paice transferred to Henley from Ashbury Crossing in 1897 and is believed to have been the first signalman to work the new signalbox at Henley station.

Courtesy Mrs. Cutbush

Henley station staff in 1921. They are from left to right: *standing:* Thomas Harker, guard; Arthur Tristem, yard foreman; Bob Lawrence, goods porter; A. Godfrey, parcel porter; - Smith, checker; - Sharp; Tom Rixon; Reg Ayres, porter, Jim Spearing; Jimmy Minall, guard; *seated:* - Rogers; Jack Record, clerk; - Baverstock, Joseph Lock, station master; C. Lock; G. L. Tranter, clerk, who later became station master of Shiplake and Wargrave; - Eustace, porter. Mr. Lock was station master from at least 1897 to 1926.

Courtesy S. Tristem

THE STAFF

Shiplake station staff c.1918. They are from left to right: *standing* Bill Whitlock, signalman; Bert Broad, lad porter; Fred East, lad porter; *seated* George Cheasley, station master, and Eddie Goodey, signalman. Mr. Cheasley retired in March 1919 after 48 years service on the GWR, 35 of which he was station master at Shiplake.

Courtesy F. I. G. Shaw

Guard T. H. Harker starting the 8.50 a.m. from Henley in 1914.

Courtesy John Harker

The Henley GWR football team of 1919. The team only played one match a year, on Good Friday at 11.00 a.m., against the GPO. It had consisted of staff from Henley station but over the years other members of staff from along the branch were involved.

Courtesy J. Jones.

Walter Ayres and his dog on the base of the old 10 ton yard crane at Henley.

Courtesy Margaret Briggs

Reg Ayres with the Parcels van in the forecourt of Henley station c.1920.

Courtesy Mr. & Mrs. V. G. Mellett

Steam railmotor No. 39 at Henley station in 1931.   *W. Y. George*

just too long for the turntable and so it was decided to screw down the brakes on the tender and ease the loco back against it in order effectively to shorten the wheelbase by the required amount. This was successful in the first instance, but almost inevitably the loco sprang out again from the tender to overhang the table by an amount sufficient to prevent the turning being completed. The branch locomotive took the 7.30 p.m. to Reading and, following about an hour's struggle to ease the engine

against the tender again without slipping off from either end of the turntable, the turning of No. 4032 was completed and the 'Castle' class 4—6—0 was pressed into service on the local branch train.

Another incident occurred on the turntable one evening, although the date has not been established, when a '43XX' class Mogul was being turned prior to working out to Reading on a passenger service. The crew mistakenly lined up the turntable with one of the pit roads instead of the buffer stop opposite the end of the siding. Consequently, the opposite end of the turntable was not aligned with the siding, and the crew, not realising this, drove the loco straight off the turntable and into the ballast.

In connection with the new road improvements between Maidenhead and Reading in 1925, the Great Western, at the request of the Berkshire County Council, agreed to construct a new road bridge, 50 ft. wide between parapets, over the Henley branch. The bridge was situated at the 32 mile post and was constructed by J. Cochrane & Sons Ltd. The work proceeded well and all of the steel work for the new bridge was erected on Sunday, 11th April 1926. The bridge was built to a traditional design using blue engineering brick and a steel plate girder span.

'517' class 0—4—2T No. 1429 at Henley on the Reading auto service c.1930. The driver, on the right, is Alfred Lovell.   *Reg Daniells*

The collection and delivery of goods in the locality had been carried out by Toomer's, the appointed agents, but, following the death of Mr. Robert Toomer in 1892, the Great Western decided to provide the service themselves. At first three horses and single horse lorries were provided at Henley, together with a 'vehicle for boats etc.' and a hand barrow. Stabling accommodation was hired and the following staff were appointed to man the new section: 1 clerk, 3 carmen, 1 vanguard and a parcels porter.

By 1895 the service was well established and the company built its own stables. This was a substantial brick structure, based on a standard GWR design, housing four horses and incorporating a cart shed for two vehicles. It

A large walnut butt shortly after arrival in the goods yard for despatch by rail in 1937. This tree was 250 years old and was purchased from Phyllis Court for £100. The uniformed member of staff is Arthur Tristem who was the yard foreman. *Courtesy Cyril Tristem*

was situated on the edge of the goods yard in a corner of the station meadow.

The service flourished and in 1898 an additional horse and cart were provided for parcels, followed by another in 1900, illustrated on page 36. However, traffic continued to increase still further and in 1906 the stables were extended to accommodate two more horses for both goods and parcels, one of them replacing a pony which was sent to Bristol as it was evidently no longer adequate for the parcels round. Another 'standard horse lorry' and parcels van were also provided at this time and an additional carman and van boy engaged.

Yet another horse, lorry and carman were added in 1908 and a parcels delivery lad in 1910, but by 1920 the trend reversed and the thriving parcels service declined markedly. The effects of road competition were becoming only too evident and the GWR, who were effecting economies at the time, handed over the delivery of local parcels to Toomer R. & Co. Ltd. who once again became the company's appointed agent.

The carman, Jimmy Jones, with his horse Sam, had worked the parcels service around the town since 1916. The businesses on which he called were issued with cards which they displayed in the window of their premises when there were any goods to collect. When this service was withdrawn Mr. Jones transferred to Twyford where he served as a lampman for some 11 years until the Great Western reinstated the parcels service in February, 1932, when he returned to Henley to take up his former position as goods carter along with F. M. Stacey from Tilehurst.

There were three horses based at Henley at this time, two of which were of a 'heavy' breed used to haul the

Jimmy Jones with his horse Sam in Duke Street, Henley. *Courtesy J. Jones*

W. Y. George

'517' class 0—4—2T No. 526 alongside the main platform at Henley in April 1931.

goods lorries, while the third, a smaller animal, was used on the much lighter parcels delivery van. The horse-drawn parcels van, then driven by W. Ayres, was soon displaced by a motor lorry which was sent to serve the outlying district and collect milk from local farms. The parcels service was then combined with 'class 3' goods deliveries and the two horse-drawn lorries continued to serve the town until after the Second World War.

Once through the main doors of the booking hall, the platforms at Henley station were open to the public and so tickets were examined at Shiplake. Of course this was a constant source of delay to 'down' trains as it could apparently take up to 7 or 8 minutes to collect the tickets from a waiting train before it could be cleared to complete its journey to Henley. It was not until 1933 that a ticket barrier was finally installed to enclose the platforms at the terminus.

The Great Western's first diesel railcar, built by AEC, was completed in December 1933. The vehicle was fitted with ATC and put into regular daily service, which included a return trip over the Henley branch. The service was to have commenced on Monday, 5th February, 1934, but it is believed that the railcar failed beforehand and in fact the service began later that week. Also in 1934 minor alterations were carried out to the track layout and signal-

ling at Henley. These included the removal of a trailing crossover from the 'down' running line to the 'down' sidings and part of the 'up' trailing connection to the same. Consequent alterations included the removal of one of the arms from the triple bracket intermediate home signal, the addition of a calling on arm to the inner home signal and route indicator boxes to the starting signals serving platforms 1 and 2. These appear to have been the first significant alterations since 1904.

The GWR stationed a camp coach at Wargrave from the mid 1930s onwards. The vehicle was stabled in the goods siding behind the station platform and was at first a small 4 berth vehicle. However, by 1939, this had been replaced with a larger vehicle with 6 berths. A camp coach was also later provided at Shiplake.

By the summer of 1937, after a satisfactory performance, railcar No. 1 had been taken off the previously mentioned service. It was replaced by a Collett 0—4—2T and auto trailer on what was said to have been one of the hardest auto turns in the country, covering some 240 miles a day from Southall to Slough, Windsor, Reading, Henley and Oxford.

Just before the Second World War, H. W. Carter, station master at Henley from December 1936 to August 1939, wrote the following description of a typical day in

'3901' class 2—6—2T No. 3915 leaving Henley in May 1931.   *W. Y. George*

his working life which was published in the *Great Western Railway Magazine* under the heading of 'Spotlight on my Job'.

A Station Master carries many and varied responsibilities, but taking it all round his position is a congenial one. As a matter of fact it is largely what he makes it. I have a splendid staff here at Henley, and believe in giving them every encouragement. Consequently we work as a team and the day's work is all the more enjoyable for that.

On the way to duty in the morning I first pass through the goods shed and office — I am responsible for goods and passenger traffic — and see that the work is well up to time. From here I go on to the passenger station where I confirm that the business trains are formed and ready, well warmed and well cleaned. This is a residential area with a good number of first class passengers, and I like to pay special attention to the trains they use.

There is little chance to look at my correspondence until the business trains are away. Then I open and read through the letters, lay aside those requiring my personal attention and distribute the rest, with any necessary instructions, to the clerks responsible.

H. W. CARTER

I now make a round of the station, stopping first to read the gas and water meters and initial the staff time-sheets. I inspect the platforms and waiting rooms, and make sure that all notices for the public are up to date. The signal box is my next call. Here I sign the train register and look through the train running for the previous day.

So much for routine. Throughout the day incoming trains have to be met and, as this is a terminal station, attention has to be paid to their prompt shunting and re-forming as outgoing trains. Before trains leave for Twyford, which is our junction with the main line, I satisfy myself that all doors are shut and handles turned; and I always try to see that our trains are away just as soon as the clock says 'go!'

At quiet periods of the day there are shopkeepers and traders to be waited on with a view to obtaining traffic, and just occasionally for the investigation of complaints. We make a strong point of keeping on the very best of terms with the townspeople. It helps them and it is a good thing for us — as our rising receipts show! This is another direction in which I am lucky with my staff. They are as 'keen as mustard' on securing new traffic.

I occasionally have a walk round the yard to see that traffic is berthed expeditiously and placed where the traders require it, and also make a general note as to the fitness of our horses and the condition of the motor lorries.

That brings me to another point. The cartage work at this station is very heavy for its size. We cover an extensive area with country lorry services, and also collect milk, morning and night. This requires constant attention. Another feature of the work at Henley is that we have storage sidings in which is stored passenger stock used for holiday services. The forming of these coaches into trains at holiday times and the washing and cleaning of stock while in store comes under my general supervision.

The word 'Henley' to many people means regatta; the word 'regatta' to us means a busy time. We collect something like 10,000 tickets over the four days.

Among notabilities who come here for the regatta is Lord (formerly Mr. Stanley) Baldwin. I have often chatted with him — a real English gentleman.

The river brings a good deal of other traffic to Henley in the form of rail and river excursions, and on Sundays fishermen are attracted by the free fishing.

County tank No. 2224 being turned at Henley prior to working a through train to Paddington in May 1931.   *W. Y. George*

A tantalizing glimpse of the branch train from Twyford passing Mill Lane box in the 1930s.   *Reg Daniells*

To end as I began — on a note of routine — the last job of the day is the signing of letters and accounts and the checking of the books. When I go home I say 'good night' to the staff in the sincere hope that no emergency will necessitate my reappearance on duty until the usual time the following morning. — H. W. CARTER, HENLEY-ON-THAMES.

The railways again fell under the control of the Government at the outbreak of the Second World War and services were immediately cut. From 3rd September, 1939, the 8.50 a.m. was the only through train from Henley to Paddington (there had been four each morning) until 5th February, 1940, when the 10.00 a.m. was reinstated.

The GWR were heavily committed with long distance evacuation trains and Government traffic, for which the larger class of tender locomotives were required, and so 2–6–2T locomotives replaced them on many services, which included the 8.48 a.m. from Henley to Paddington. Henley is thought to have received at least two trains of evacuees who were billeted in the town.

The railways were generally hard pressed with the war effort and, whilst the Henley branch was not directly involved, the line was busy enough under normal circumstances and further stretched when a considerable number of Londoners who could afford to do so moved out of the City and commuted to London each day. These 'voluntary evacuees' filled the through trains from Henley to capacity and, certainly by the time they reached Twyford, additional passengers boarding the train had to stand for the rest of the journey to Paddington.

Because of the wartime needs, very few coaches were stored at Henley during 1940 although some 15 LMS vehicles, the first known to have been stored there other than very occasional half-day excursions, were kept there for several weeks.

One particular frustration to travellers making the short journey from Reading to Henley each evening at this time (and apparently even up until 1952) was that after the 4.30 p.m. departure, the next train to Twyford was not until 5.45 p.m. This frequently did not actually depart until about 6.00 p.m. and all too often meant that it was held outside Twyford while the 5.15 p.m. from Paddington to Henley, with which it was supposed to connect, crossed over the 'up' relief on its way to Henley, thus leaving the Henley passengers from Reading with a long wait at Twyford for the next branch train.

With the blackout in force such station lighting that continued was subdued 'blue lighting', achieved by painting the illuminated glasses with blue paint, and lighting generally was only provided under covered areas. Shades were fitted to strategically placed platform lamps in order that they might continue to be used, and, as an additional safety precaution, white lines were reintroduced along the edges of the platforms.

Station nameboards were removed in 1940 as it was thought there was a danger that they might have been of assistance to low flying enemy aircraft or enemy troops in the event of an invasion. This made it necessary for the names of the stations to be called out to passengers of arriving trains.

Also in 1941 there was a general withdrawal of first class accommodation from London suburban trains and the facility was not restored at Henley until 7th October, 1946.

For a short time during the war, a special three coach train was stabled at Wargrave each night. The train provided living accommodation for Sir James Milne, the General Manager of the GWR, and was stabled at the end of the goods yard together with the loco which remained there overnight on standby. The train left for London each morning but its presence in the siding prevented the branch goods from putting off wagons there on its way down the branch to Henley, so during these few weeks the

A quiet scene at Henley on Saturday 30th August 1947.

R. F. Roberts

A variety of coaching stock at Henley in 1947. Many of the vehicles stored here were wartime casualties awaiting attention.

Pat Garland

wagons for Wargrave had to be taken on to the terminus and left on the return journey when the special train had gone.

Ambulance trains were often run into Henley first thing in the morning before the branch goods. Among those conveyed were many wounded from D-Day landings, bound for a hospital at Kingwood Common. They were collected from the station in service vehicles. Such trains went mainly unrecorded but on two occasions in 1944 they were doubleheaded by LNER 'B12' class 4–6–0 No. 8518 and GWR No. 6828 *Trellech Grange* on 8th August, and another LNER 'B12' No. 8579, again with *Trellech Grange* on 16th August. Ambulance trains continued to run after the war and in 1946 at least one brought prisoners of war to the town who were held in a camp at Badgemore.

The Great Western Railway Company was brought to an end when the railways in the country came under public ownership on 1st January, 1948, at which time they were taken over by the Railway Executive of the British Transport Commission.

Prior to this, during the last years of Great Western ownership, various minor improvements were carried out on the branch. At the end of the war, in fact probably not long after VE day, the semi-circular booking office at Henley, which had stood inside the new entrance hall facing passengers as they entered the station, was moved across the hall and in effect tucked away behind and between the main doors. This move was carried out in order that the office could be illuminated by daylight from the two windows in the front of the station. The toplights in the roof of the booking hall were quite inadequate to illuminate the office which had been totally dependent on gas lighting.

In 1947 the GWR introduced a zonal delivery service. The scheme involved dividing the country into areas, each with its own railhead and sub-railheads. Basically, it set out to provide a next day delivery for 'smalls' and miscellaneous goods traffic mainly by eliminating trans-shipment. As sub-railheads performed the cartage of smaller stations, traffic was concentrated at fewer loading points, which made more direct wagons possible. Sub-railheads and railheads were also linked by 'trunk motors'.

The branch came under No. 15 area, the railhead for which was Reading, with Henley as a sub-railhead covering some '8 miles distant'. As part of this scheme the loading facilities at Henley were improved by the provision of canopies over the existing loading platforms at either end of the goods shed. The canopies were clad with corrugated asbestos sheeting but were not the first sign of post-war economical modernisation. A new bicycle shed also constructed of this material was provided at Wargrave at the beginning of 1946 and two years later a similar structure was provided at Henley.

The year 1947 also marked the retirement of James Minall, a guard on the line, who at the age of 71 had become the oldest guard in the London Division. Jimmy, as he was known, had served 48 years on the branch, having started at Henley as a porter in 1898. He was a well-known character and prided himself in always wearing a buttonhole which he renewed daily for 45 years. When he ran short, one of his friends at Shiplake apparently tied a posy to a hoop which was handed to him as the train

Jimmy Minall logging the name of the loco crew at Paddington prior to working his last train to Henley.

Courtesy Mrs. K. Broadbent

passed over the level crossing. He retired on the 23rd March and for his last twelve years at Henley had worked the 8.48 a.m. to Paddington.

An entertaining incident indirectly concerning one of the through trains from Paddington to Henley was recalled by the late J. N. Maskelyne and appeared in the *Model Railway News* for August 1948:

And now I am reminded of an amusing incident which happened one evening not so long ago; amusing that is, to you and me now, but not so amusing to the train crews and the passengers concerned in it. On the said evening something went wrong with the brakes of the 6.25 p.m. fast train from Paddington to Twyford and Henley, and the train was unable to start. Paddington decided to let the 6.30 p.m. West of England express go first, and duly sent a message to this effect down the line. A Relief signalman was on duty in Twyford East Box, and either he did not receive the message, or he misunderstood it. Anyway when he was offered the 6.30 express, he thought it was the 6.25 and duly set the crossover from main to relief roads and offered a branch train to Twyford West who promptly set the road for the Henley branch. The Result. The express duly arrived, and its driver probably not without surprise, found the Twyford distant signal against him and the road set for crossing over from main to relief. The lordly King and its crack express took the crossover at the regulation 35 mph, sailed majestically through Twyford station, found the signals off for the Henley line and was engine and five coaches round the branch before he could stop! Let us draw a veil over the subsequent proceedings. The language is unprintable. I will merely add that to enable the express to resume its normal route, a considerable amount of manoeuvring was required, due chiefly to the fact that the 6.25 train, by this time, had arrived at Twyford East box and was waiting to cross from Main to Relief on its way to Henley.

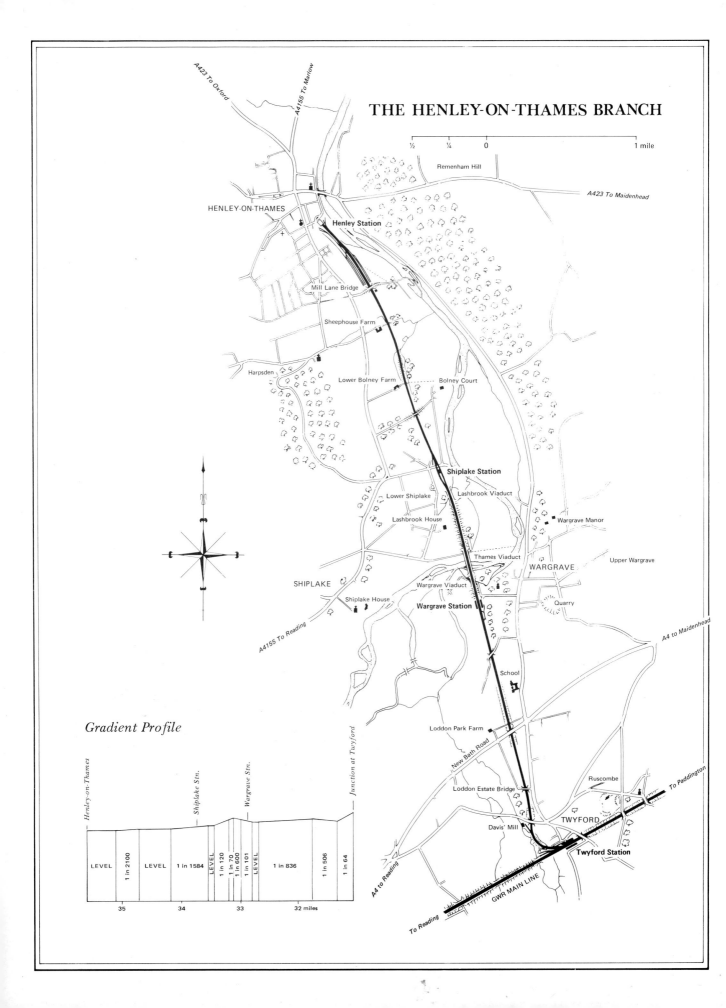

THE HENLEY-ON-THAMES BRANCH

½   ¼   0   1 mile

A423 To Oxford
A4155 To Marlow
Remenham Hill
A423 To Maidenhead

HENLEY-ON-THAMES
Henley Station

Mill Lane Bridge
Sheephouse Farm

Harpsden
Lower Bolney Farm
Bolney Court

Shiplake Station
Lower Shiplake
Lashbrook Viaduct
Lashbrook House
Wargrave Manor

SHIPLAKE
Thames Viaduct
Upper Wargrave
WARGRAVE

Wargrave Viaduct
Shiplake House
Wargrave Station
Quarry

A4155 To Reading
A4 to Maidenhead

School

Loddon Park Farm

New Bath Road
Ruscombe
To Paddington

Loddon Estate Bridge
TWYFORD
Davis' Mill
Twyford Station

A4 to Reading
GWR MAIN LINE
To Reading

Gradient Profile

Henley-on-Thames
Shiplake Stn.
Wargrave Stn.
Junction at Twyford

| LEVEL | 1 in 2100 | LEVEL | 1 in 1584 | LEVEL | 1 in 120 | 1 in 70 | 1 in 600 | 1 in 101 | LEVEL | 1 in 836 | 1 in 506 | 1 in 64 |

35   34   33   32 miles

CHAPTER FIVE

THE LINE DESCRIBED

Part 1: Along the route

ALTHOUGH the railway itself has changed, at the time of writing it is still possible to journey along the line to Henley and enjoy the beauty of much of the unspoilt Thames countryside through which it passes. The photographs in this chapter wherever possible show the branch before the removal of the 'down' running line but the following account describes the branch as it is today, with constant reference to features that no longer exist but which survived into the early 1950s, when the branch remained intact and relatively unchanged since the early 1900s.

Until recent years the Henley branch commenced from a double junction with the main line at Twyford station, 31 miles 4 chains from Paddington. Local trains still depart from the No. 5 bay platform, which is tucked away behind the west end of the 'up' relief platform. This bay was equipped with an engine release crossover that was used by the branch locomotive when running round to the other end of its train.

The end of the branch platform curves away from the main line and the branch itself continues to curve sharply northwards, falling away from the station on a 1 in 64 falling grade on a high embankment, crossing the narrow

access road that led to the goods yard and a backwater of the River Loddon by means of a blue brick arch bridge and culvert respectively. A platelayers hut is situated at the foot of the embankment between these two bridges and further to the east the line overlooks St. Mary's Church and the terraced housing development of Brook Street, which reaches down to the edge of the backwater. This housing development dates from the late 1870s. In fact Twyford owes much of its extension and development to the coming of the railway, before which most of its housing was concentrated along the London and Bath main road.

The private siding serving Twyford mill ran alongside the 'down' line, flanked by young trees on the outside of the curve, before the backwater was recrossed by another culvert, immediately after which the siding turned away through a wooden gate and into the mill premises. This siding was connected to the 'up' line of the branch by means of a trailing connection that commenced near the foot of the station platform, just short of the branch's own connection with the 'up' relief line. The siding was originally connected to the branch by means of a facing point that was situated just outside the mill, but this

Railcar No. 1 in the Henley branch bay at Twyford on Saturday 30th August 1947.   *R. F. Roberts*

0—6—0PT No. 5766 passing Wargrave Piggot School with a branch train for Twyford on 22nd September 1951.

J. F. Russell-Smith

Looking towards Henley, showing the original wrought iron bridge carrying the High Street over the line. *P. J. Garland*

The Loddon Estate bridge. *Author*

arrangement was probably altered when the line was doubled.

At the end of the severe curve, just past the mill, the gradient eases to 1 in 506 and iron railings fence off the Polehampton Boys School which is passed on the east immediately before the bridge carrying the High Street over the railway. This school had the misfortune of being situated right alongside the railway and suffered the inevitable distractions caused by passing trains. Not surprisingly, the school complained, and in despair during the line's heyday the children were given a half day's holiday throughout the duration of the special regatta traffic.

The bridge here was one of the original structures with wrought iron plate girders which survived until 1968, when it was rebuilt with prestressed concrete beams. Immediately after this, in a steep cutting, the direction of the line's curve reverses for a short distance before commencing the straight course that is held until the other side of the River Thames. The cutting gradually

lessens until after the line passes under the Loddon Estate bridge, after which it runs virtually at ground level overlooking the gardens of the residential properties that were erected on the Loddon Park Estate, past a platelayers hut on the 'up' side, before heading into open country.

The down grade lessens to 1 in 836 and a shallow cutting, beginning around the 31¾ mile post, takes the line up to the new A4 Twyford bypass for which the modern steel plate girder bridge, at 32 miles, was specially constructed in 1926. After this bridge the 'up' fixed distant for Twyford, together with a fogman's hut and occupation crossing were left behind and the line

The A4 bridge with the fixed distant for Twyford and fogman's hut in the foreground. *D. J. Hyde*

Wargrave Lane occupation bridge.   *N. de Courtais*

crosses the Wargrave Parish boundary. This occupation crossing had maintained what was once the only means of access to Twyfordfield (later Loddon Park) Farm.

Still in a shallow cutting, the branch skirts the edge of the playing fields of the Wargrave Piggot School, which is situated to the east of the line and enjoys greater detachment from the once busy traffic than the boys' school at Twyford. The cutting ends just past the school and the

line continues at ground level through flat agricultural land towards Wargrave. Immediately before the Wargrave Lane occupation bridge, at 32 miles 41 chains, another platelayers hut once stood on the 'up' side of the line, situated between a culvert that runs under the line at this point and the embankment of the eastern approach to the bridge.

Through the bridge the line, flanked by pine trees to the east, passed a simple goods yard that was also situated on the eastern side of the line, before entering Wargrave station at 32 miles 68 chains. The land to the west of the company's boundary is completely open, affording an uninterrupted view over the continuing cultivated land.

In marked contrast to the layouts of Shiplake and Henley which evolved over a number of years, the station at Wargrave, having been built so late in the line's history, had a distinctly planned appearance. As mentioned earlier, the main station building and waiting room stood on opposite facing platforms, connected by a covered footbridge, and what was once a quiet shady lane still leads from the edge of the station forecourt to the village.

In 1881, before the station was built, it was recorded in the *Henley & Remenham Record* that a train from Twyford became stuck in a snow drift just before reaching the Thames Viaduct, presumably near the station site. The incident occurred in the early evening of Tuesday, 18th January. The snow had begun only that morning and did not cease until the Thursday afternoon. The passengers,

A Henley train approaching Wargrave in May 1956.   *J. A. Fleming*

Wargrave station on 19th July 1958.   *Pat Moffatt*

Looking towards the Thames viaduct from Wargrave station footbridge.   *Pat Moffatt*

The main spans of the Thames viaduct from the east.   *Author*

The line of trees screening the viaduct from view.   *J. M. Judge*

Looking towards Wargrave along the embankment that joins the Thames and Lashbrook viaducts.   *Pat Moffatt*

who included those from the London slip coach, struggled back to Twyford, and the branch service was suspended until the train was dug out on Thursday afternoon.

The line leaves the north end of the station on a substantial embankment, on the first rising gradient of 1 in 101, crossing a minor road and flood stream by means of a modest blue brick arch viaduct, at 33 m. 0½ ch., known as Wargrave Viaduct, on the approach to the Thames.

The river is crossed by the largest engineering feature on the line, an eleven span viaduct consisting of wrought iron plate girders resting on both blue brick and cast iron pillars. The gradient of the line changes part way across this structure from a rising gradient of 1 in 600 to fall away at 1 in 120 towards Shiplake.

This structure provides a splendid view of the Thames, and this was particularly so in earlier years before the trees alongside had grown.

Looking west along the river, the viaduct overlooks Shiplake Lock while to the east the river can be seen curving gently downstream towards Henley as it disappears across the rich open pasture land of the flood plain, with densely forested hills in the distance beyond. This inspiring view was of course for many excursionists the first sight of the beautiful riverside surroundings which they had travelled to see, perhaps bound for a cruise on the river or a simple stroll along its banks.

For the loco crews on a hot summer's day, a cool breeze from the river was refreshing and a welcome relief from the confined heat of the cab, but it was quite a different story in the winter, when cruel winds blew across the viaduct. This was particularly gruelling for the crews of locomotives with open cabs, and one of the branch drivers claimed it was so cold that at times he had felt that his face would have cracked if he'd spoken.

The beauty of the Thames and its surroundings are carefully protected, as became evident during the proposed extension of the railway to Marlow when one of the letters of protest at the time referred to the viaduct as 'an eyesore'. The GWR were obviously under some pressure over the appearance of the new structure as drawings were in fact prepared showing less 'basic' designs, but in the event, the plans for the present structure were adhered to and the completed bridge was simply screened from view by a row of trees specially planted along the flood plain on the eastern side of the viaduct.

Once across the river, having left Berkshire, the line continues through the county of Oxfordshire on what is undoubtedly the more attractive part of the route, almost parallel to the course of the river. Commencing on a high embankment, past the site of a platelayers hut that had stood at the top on the 'up' side of the line, the railway continues on a level course towards Shiplake across rich and often water-logged meadows on the edge of the flood plain. With Lashbrook Farm to the west, the Shiplake 'down' distant was passed and at the end of a small spinney surrounding a pond on the eastern boundary, the line falls again at 1 in 1584 as it turns gently westwards. The second farm occupation crossing is known as Knights Crossing, the approaches to which are inclined to reach the top of the embankment. The crossing, protected with 'whistle' boards erected some 500 yards either side of it, was the scene of an accident which took place in the fog at 7.20 in the morning of 7th June 1941. A light engine travelling to Henley ran into a herd of cattle that were being driven over the crossing. Seven of the animals were killed and another put down as a result of injuries.

The river is just visible across the meadows to the east and immediately before entering Shiplake station the line crosses the Lashbrook stream by means of a low viaduct that is virtually a much scaled down version of the Thames viaduct, being similar in both construction and appearance.

Lashbrook viaduct from the east.   *Author*

The first of the six spans of this structure accommodates an under-line farm crossing that, certainly today, appears to duplicate Knights Crossing.

The 'down' line diverged at the end of the viaduct to run along the westernmost face of the island platform at Shiplake. The station is situated on the continuing down grade of 1 in 1584 and consists of a single platform formerly located between the 'up' and 'down' running lines and on which the station building still stands. The footbridge which spanned the site gave access to the platform, at the end of which was a traditional level crossing and a simple goods yard connected to the 'down' line only by means

An 'up' branch train preparing to leave Shiplake in the 1950s.   *F. I. G. Shaw*

of a trailing connection. Throughout the site the line is more or less at ground level, the platform itself being bounded to the west with what was a grazing meadow and a few houses and to the east by the gardens of larger residential properties.

At the northern end of the station a public footpath crosses the line at the neck of the goods yard, close to which is another sleeper built platelayers hut. The line then passes the large glasshouses of a nursery adjoining the western boundary of the railway as it leaves the outskirts of the quiet village, on a straight course, past the fashionable riverside properties that were constructed on the east side of the line during the early part of this century.

Shortly after the 34 mile post, the line levels out and a 'whistle' board for the next occupation crossing preceded the most attractive overbridge on the line, carrying the private drive to Bolney Court over the railway by means of a splendid cast iron lattice girder span, supported on red brick jack arches. A brick built platelayers hut was tucked away at the foot of the embankment carrying the eastern approach to this structure.

Immediately after this bridge the line curves gently northwards across further rich meadowland on the final approach to Henley. This stretch of the branch may perhaps escape the attention of many travellers for the river is distant to the east and obscured from view. However, to my mind, the rustic pastures that extend from its banks epitomise the gracious and seemingly timeless landscape of the Thames around Henley.

Willow trees flank the railway's eastern boundary before reaching a spinney that extends alongside the railway for over a quarter of a mile. The 'up' distant signal for Shiplake

The more ornate lattice girdered Bolney bridge, another original structure which still survives. *Author*

The P.W. hut by Bolney bridge. *A. E. Smith*

My favourite stretch of the line looking through the willows towards Henley from Bolney bridge. *Reg Daniells*

0—6—0PT No. 5763 approaching Bolney bridge with a branch train from Henley on 14th June 1951. The absence of any headcode was not unusual on this line!

J. F. Russell-Smith

The Henley fixed distant just south of Sheephouse Farm crossing.

Pat Moffatt

stood alongside this spinney just south of the occupation crossing at Lower Bolney Farm. As already mentioned, this crossing was again protected by 'whistle' boards and, until 1961, fitted with a warning bell. The footpath over the line at this spot had been maintained by an attractive wooden footbridge that was ideally suited to the delightful surroundings. The structure only survived until 3rd April 1921, at which time it was removed, but a drawing of this appears on page 14.

Because the line at this point is still not very far from the river, the land to the east of the line is liable to flooding. The trees in the spinney are mainly willow and silver birch and, with the ground being particularly waterlogged here, marsh marigolds can often be seen in the spring, growing alongside the track at the foot of the low embankment which commences at the 34½ mile post.

The end of the spinney is marked by the last of three successive culverts that occur after the crossing and the line takes the final, although hardly apparent, down grade of 1 in 2112, as it passes another sleeper built platelayers hut on the 'down' side and resumes the level of the surrounding open farm land.

Sheephouse Farm Crossing, shortly after the fixed distant signal for Henley and the 34¾ mile post, saw frequent use by the farmer and in addition to the usual 'whistle' boards was equipped with 'tremulous bells' to give extra warning of approaching trains. The location of

this crossing was easily identified by the row of tall elm trees that used to grow from east to west alongside the approaches before Dutch elm disease took its toll.

Much of this stretch of the branch, from Bolney Bridge to Mill Lane, can in fact be seen at a distance from the Henley to Reading road.

The P.W. gang at work on the 'down' line near the Sheephouse Farm crossing c.1959. The lookout has not been identified, but the sub ganger on the right is W. T. Hughes.

Courtesy B. W. Hughes

Looking back towards Sheephouse Farm crossing from Mill Lane bridge.   *Pat Moffatt*

to the bank of the River Thames. This was apparent on either side of the carriage sidings, at the neck of which the station was bounded to the west by private coal and timber yards, and to the east by a public footpath and Cold Bath Stream, both of which were further bounded by a screen of trees that still hide the railway from the riverside promenade. Before the 1920s, when the site was developed, the land occupied by the promenade had been low lying with numerous water channels.

The much lengthened platforms of the station extended from the original timber overall roof beneath which the line terminated. Other facilities there included a simple but lengthy goods yard, and an engine shed and turntable.

The final approach to Henley continues through open farmland on the gentle down grade, past the former crossing keeper's house, alongside which stood Mill Lane signal box, before finally levelling out under Mill Lane Bridge to emerge between the numerous carriage sidings at the southern end of the terminus.

Henley station itself is situated amidst and level with what had been mainly lush grazing land that extended

Today it would be difficult for a visitor arriving at Henley station to even imagine how the station had once appeared let alone to appreciate the highly individual character of a country terminus that for much of the working day had accommodated long trains headed by main line express locomotives and yet in quieter moments so often seemed little more than a minor branch line served by a small pannier tank and two coaches.

The branch train crossing over from the 'down' line on arrival at Henley in 1958.   *Arthur Hearn*

Part 2: The Stations

HENLEY-ON-THAMES

66

These two aerial views featuring Henley station in May 1920 and July 1957 respectively, clearly show the position of the station in relation to both the town and river. The finish of the regatta course can also be seen to the north of the famous bridge. *Aerofilms*

A late 1920s view of Station Road looking towards the station. The row of trees remain from the original boundary of Station Meadow shown opposite. This road, built by the GWR, was originally gated and closed to the public each evening about 9.00-9.30 p.m. It was taken over by the local council in 1877 and widened, as illustrated, in 1926. The iron railings (repositioned here) enclosing the meadow date from 1907 when they replaced the post and wire fencing (just discernible on page 36) at a cost of £55. A hoarding in Station Meadow evidently aroused some local objections as, following a fire of a quantity of waste paper there in March 1931, during which it appeared that the hoardings might be destroyed, the local newspaper was moved to report that 'such hopes were not to be realized and they still stand as conspicuous and disfiguring as ever'! The road that leads on to Henley bridge was a later addition built by some of the town's 'poor men' in 1862. It was financed by the workhouse fund, one of the town's charities, for the total cost of £126.

Courtesy Henley Town Council

A later view of the station entrance during the early 1960s showing the modified canopy valancing. The single name board facing the river was a later GWR addition which survived until at least 1961, after which it was replaced with two Western Region chocolate and cream enamel signs that were erected at either end of the canopy. The small gateway in the iron railings led through to the loco yard alongside the station and was the only means of access for the loco crews after the station was locked each night. The advertisement hoardings alongside were a later addition thought to date from the 1930s. The small confectioner's shop alongside the station was built in 1923 and until about 1954 was occupied by Messrs. D. A. Ritter after which the business was taken over by Mr. Shephard. There was also a small snack bar run by Mrs. Lay from a grounded radar van that was set back from the pavement, in between the end of the iron railings and the shop.

Lens of Sutton

The new entrance hall contained a semi-circular booking office which, as already mentioned, was enclosed with polished oak panelling and before 1945 had backed against the wall enclosing the overall roof, facing towards the main entrances. After this time, it was moved across the hall and tucked away behind the main doors. The two apertures that can be seen at either end of the far wall, against which the weighing machine is standing, were situated immediately opposite the main entrance doors and led through from the booking hall into the old station and under the large overall roof. The entrance hall, concourse and platforms were paved throughout and, before erection of the ticket barriers during 1933, the platforms were open to the public, tickets being checked while the passengers were captive at Shiplake. Incidentally, platform tickets were introduced at Henley in 1915. The bookstall was originally leased by Messrs. W. H. Smith as seen on page 131. In this view it is seen during the early 1950s occupied by Messrs. Wyman's. The main gate, on the right of the picture, was manned by a ticket collector who was provided with the timber built ticket collector's box alongside (also illustrated opposite). This was fitted with stable doors and equipped with a ticket rack and the usual tall wooden stool. In practice, the ticket gate on the left of the picture normally remained locked and was only brought into use during the regatta.

British Railways

This photograph was taken from the westernmost entrance from the booking hall, looking into the main station on 25th March, 1961.

D. Thompson

Looking towards the ticket barrier from the main platform in 1965. The buffer stops were screened with varnished timber panels that each bore four mounted and glazed photographs of classic scenes showing places of interest or beauty served by the GWR. The buffer stops themselves were perhaps somewhat unusual in bearing spring loaded buffers. The top of the bookstall can be seen behind and to the right of the ticket collector's box. The staff room, situated to the right just out of the picture, was provided beneath the verandah in 1907. The loop siding still projecting through the north end of the roof on a 1904 plan, was probably shortened at that time and the original aperture sealed with brick. The platform had also been extended across the end of the siding and the new room was simply achieved by enclosing the resultant space with timber panelling at a cost of £69.

A. E. Smith

The platforms were renumbered when the station signs were replaced under BR ownership, the No. 3 bay and No. 1 platform numbers being transposed. Platform No. 2 was officially recognised as the arrival platform and No. 1 as the departure. The wooden nameboards with their cast iron lettering, illustrated here during the early 1950s, were replaced with the stove enamelled signs seen in the previous view. The accommodation of the station building to the left of the picture was as follows: Gentlemen's lavatories, store (previously bicycles), both of which were in the foreground just out of the picture, waiting room, ladies' room, parcels office and cloakroom, the latter with stable type doors, and, beyond the ticket barrier, the station master's office. Footwarmer heating apparatus was provided in 1883 at a cost of £16, but where this was housed has not been established. The overall roof only accommodated about one and a half coaches of the long through trains to Paddington and naturally tended to shield the station from the steady bark of the locomotives departing with these trains. Consequently, the rear vehicles of such departures left quite silently and seemed to just glide out into the sunlight, leaving only the familiar odour of burning lamp oil that always lingered there.

S. Fletcher

The smoke troughs were probably added when the northern end of the roof was enclosed during the 1904 improvements. They were shallow and in practice often proved quite inadequate to cope with the smoke emitted from locomotives, especially on damp days when the roof filled with smoke and gave cause for complaint. The branch crews frequently made a point of stopping with the chimney directly under one of the shafts in an attempt to avoid the problem.

A. E. Smith

No. 5038 *Morlais Castle* in platform No. 2 shortly after arrival with the 5.20 p.m. from Paddington on Friday, 14th June, 1963, the last day of steam hauled through trains between Henley and London.

P. Moffatt

The timber columns supporting the east side of the main roof had obviously rotted at some stage and were consequently cut off above ground level and supported on lengths of angle iron, sunk into new concrete foundations. Two of the columns were supported on lengths of old Barlow rail from the Broad Gauge. The roof extended over the loop siding which was enclosed by a long brick wall against the other side of which the engine shed was built. This enclosure, officially referred to as 'the verandah', was mostly screened from the platforms by large advertisement hoardings mounted on the timber columns. This siding was used to stable the branch coaches but had formerly been part of the run round loop that extended right through the station to the original turntable. The engine release crossover alongside what had become platform No. 3 was operated by the 2-lever ground frame just inside the roof. This frame dated from the 1904 alterations and was released by lever No. 50 (No. 34 following the 1956 alterations) in the signal box. A telephone was provided alongside for communication between the shunter and signalman.

Photoscript — Deddington

Looking back at the station in 1954 with the local branch train in the platform. The corrugated asbestos bicycle shed on the left was provided during the early part of 1948.

I. D. Beale

72

A classic view of the station in 1951 clearly showing the platform canopy that was erected in 1904. The GWR paint scheme illustrated here is thought to date from the late 1930s and the obvious repair to the glazed gable effected about the same time. The station was repainted in the Western Region colours of chocolate and cream in July 1956.

M. W. Earley

0—6—0PT No. 4606 gently backs on to the two coach branch train to form the 3.02 p.m. to Twyford on 5th May, 1956.

Brian Wright

The same loco being coupled to the train. Generally on arrival the branch train ran right into the station just short of the buffers. When the train was empty the coaches were pushed back out from under the roof to clear the release crossover in order that the loco could run round to the other end of the train. The coaches were then pushed back under the roof. However, when time was short, arriving trains merely stopped short of the crossover.

Brian Wright

Looking towards the station in 1947 from the throat of the loco yard. The loco coal wagon can just be seen in its usual position, the wagon being moved along to the beginning of the siding when required for coaling. The branch loco was so positioned on the turntable siding that the coal could be shovelled directly into the bunker. About once a month one of these wagons was returned from Henley loaded with ashes.

J. H. Russell

It is not clear when the engine shed was built as the original plans for the station show a very different structure with a hipped roof; it is therefore a possibility that the brick building here replaced an earlier timber built broad gauge shed, but this has not been established. This building was itself originally shorter, the side wall illustrated on the opposite page only in fact extending the length of the first five sections. The larger and rearmost section was added after 1897, most probably during the 1904 improvements. The structure originally had an internal length of 58′6″ x 20′ wide, a slate roof, full length smoke trough, 44′8″ long pit and a small sand furnace which was out of use by 1897. There had also been a rough pit outside at that time but this was later filled in. The south end of the building was enclosed with a timber gable and large hinged double doors to the right of which was a staff access door and to the left a small window. When the shed was extended the timber gable was retained but the northern end, of which nothing is known of the original, was enclosed with a red brick end wall and double doors. The track terminated inside the building with small iron wheel scotches similar to those illustrated on the edge of the turntable. The overall length of the extended building totalled some 80 ft.

Pat Moffatt

One of the very few views of the shed that have been discovered, this one being taken over the fence from the Cold Bath footpath during the late 1950s. In this photograph, where the smoke trough had originally projected above the main entrance to the shed, there appears to have been a small window.

A. Attewell

The rear of the engine shed with the roof removed immediately prior to demolition and showing another staff access door in one of the main double doors. The male staff lavatories, to the right and out of the picture, were built against the side of the station, again probably in 1904. These lavatories were opened for public use during the regatta each year, access being via the small gateway shown in the lower photograph on page 67.

Author

The 55 ft modern balanced turntable was installed in 1903 to replace the smaller 45 ft diameter turntable situated at the end of the main platform. Certainly since the 1920s the table was not used anything like as much as it had been as locomotives on the London through trains were turned at Reading. The table was apparently reputed to have been cracked and, although 4—4—0 and 2—6—0 classes turned well, the larger 4—6—0s, which incidentally were watered first to help to balance the turntable, generally required a good deal of effort. It was possible for a very carefully positioned 'Hall' class loco to be turned by its own crew simply by pushing hard but most men remember using pinchbars to move the table, except of course during the regatta service when there would be five or six men available to help each other. The turntable would accommodate 'Star' class 4—6—0s but not the slightly larger 'Castle' class locos. This photograph, taken in 1947, also illustrates the rear of the handsome brick office that was built in 1904 for Messrs. Toomers, and the backs of the large advertisement hoardings that screened the yard from the road.

J. H. Russell

The water tower appears to have been one of the original structures and supported a large iron tank that additionally supplied three other water cranes as well as the station supply. It was originally open-topped, as illustrated on page 128, and official records state that it was approximately 21' above rail level measuring 17' 9" x 13' 9" x 4' 9" high, with a capacity (at 4' 6" deep) of 6,862 gallons. The building was substantially constructed of red brick and originally housed a coal platform that measured 12' 11" x 13' 5". The coal platform was out of use by 1897 by which time and thereafter the branch locos were simply coaled directly from loco coal wagons. Before being extended, the engine shed was equipped with a bunk against the westernmost wall just inside the entrance. However, this was later removed, again probably in 1904, and the disused platform of the water tower was enclosed with timber panelling, equipped with a stove and served as a mess room where the overnight shedman slept on the floor. A small hut, illustrated on page 74, was provided after the war and situated between the coal and turntable sidings. This building was intended for use as a general mess room for both enginemen and carriage cleaners and the enclosure beneath the water tank became a carriage cleaners' stores. The base of the water tower served as a loco store which was equipped with a bench and a vice and used to store fire lighters, asbestos packing, cotton waste, oil and paraffin, etc. The small cabinet alongside the entrance to the stores housed the switch gear for the electric pump and the lean-to at the rear served as the senior driver's office which also housed the meters for the station's electricity supply. When the water level was low in the tank the bell housing often failed to seat properly after use so the driver was frequently seen climbing into the tank to dislodge any fouling waste, although sometimes a tug on the release chain would shut off the supply. The brazier alongside was kept burning during the winter months to warm the leather bag which would otherwise have frozen rigid to the wastepipe.

The water tower was supplied from a 20 ft deep well alongside, water being pumped into the tank by a small 2 cylinder steam pump housed in the corrugated iron shed on the bank. The corrug-

ated iron structure replaced an earlier timber built shed on the same site. The original building had a gable roof and inside dimensions of 10' 6" long, 6' 6" wide, 7' 0" high to the wall plate and 8' 6" to the ridge. The pumping engine was powered by steam from the branch loco by means of a rigid pipe that swivelled out from a point just under the eaves and was connected in place of one of the whistles. The lower photograph shows 0—6—0PT No. 7754 coupled to the apparatus. The positioning of the loco alongside was obviously very critical in order to make the connection but eventually, after the Second World War, a flexible pipe was provided instead and simply connected to the lance cock. There was also a standby Pulsometer pump in the well but as this took some two hours to fill the tank, as opposed to the more usual 45 minutes taken by the pumping engine, it was seldom used and later, about 1950, was replaced with an electric pump. Whilst the latter saved the crews a tremendous amount of trouble, the original pumping engine was retained as a standby until the removal of the water facilities. *Photos: Pat Garland and R. Daniells*

This view shows the pump house alongside the water tower in 1959. At one time driver Albert Gardener grew chrysanthemums on the bank alongside the pump house and these could be admired from the station platforms. *Photoscript — Deddington*

Another look back at the station on 18th June, 1949, with a through train in platform No. 2., the two coach branch train alongside platform No. 1 and 0—6—0PT No. 9763 outside the shed. *J. H. Meredith*

Toomer's Coal Office

Turntable

Well
Pump House

Water Tower

35½

GWR Boundary Post

Water Crane

S.P.

Gents Lavatory

Porters Room

Booking Hall

Bookstall

Booking Office

Weighing Machine

Engine Shed

P L A T F O R M

L.P.

Disc

P L A T F O R M

L.P.

S.P.

Disc

Station Master's Office
Parcels and Cloakroom
Ladies Waiting Room

Gents Lavatory

General Waiting Room

L O A D I N G
P L A T F O R M

Cattle Pen

Coal

Loading Gauge

Weighbridge Office

Weighing Machine

10 Ton Crane 20' 6" Radius

Goods Shed

2 Ton Crane
Radius 12' 3"

Petrol

Petrol

T I M B E R
Y A R D

COAL YARD

Stables

S T A T I O N   R O A D

A L L O T M E N T S

Station Master's House

A

GWR Boundary Post

35¼

GWR Boundary Post

Disc

S.P.

Disc

A

A

0   1   2   3   4   5   CHAINS

HENLEY-ON-THAMES 1920 track plan

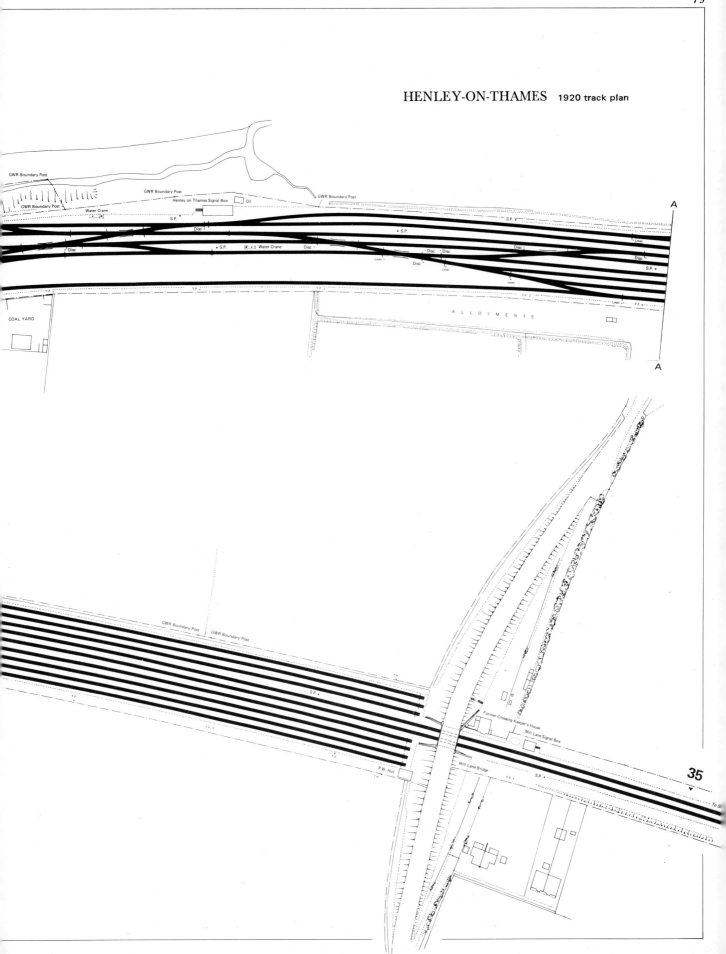

GWR Boundary Post

GWR Boundary Post

GWR Boundary Post

GWR Boundary Post

Henley on Thames Signal Box

Oil

Water Crane

S.P.

A

S.P.

Disc

S.P.

Lever

Disc

S.P.

Water Crane

Disc

Disc

Disc

Disc

Lever

Disc

Disc

Lever

Lever

Disc

S.P.

COAL YARD

A L L O T M E N T S

T.P.

T.P.

T.P.

T.P.

Lever

T.P.

A

GWR Boundary Post

GWR Boundary Post

S.P.

T.P.

Former Crossing Keeper's House

Mill Lane Signal Box

T.P.

P.W. Hut

Mill Lane Bridge

S.P.

35

To S.

The goods yard was situated to the west of the station and is seen here from the station forecourt. The weighbridge, recovered from Paddington Goods Depot, and red brick office were provided in 1920. The original weighing maching and office were provided about 1905 and situated in the goods yard to the south of the crane. The station forecourt was probably first enclosed in 1877 when the gated station road was handed over to the local council. When it was opened out again, probably about 1904, the goods yard was simultaneously enclosed with a fence occupying the line of the one illustrated in the foreground of this view. In the 1920s this fence was repositioned at the end of the station building to enclose the new weighbridge but put back to the position shown in later years when the main forecourt was also enclosed again.

P. Moffatt

The station forecourt in 1954, showing the carefully matched extension at this end of the station building. The tall chimneys were very distinctive but at some time before the Great War the one serving the parcels office caused considerable damage to the roof of the building when the top of it was blown off in a high gale. The overall roof also suffered damage from the high winds at the time. The chimneys were originally far shorter and were extended to rise above the level of the main roof, presumably to improve draughting. Milk traffic was brought in independently from local farms and loaded on to the train from the bank in the foreground. The railway later provided a motor lorry and established a daily collection round for the milk which was loaded into 'Siphon' vans and taken to London.

I. D. Beale

The goods shed was a handsome building of some character with Gothic style apertures and substantial buttressing at each corner. It was constructed of red brick with stone dressings and a slate roof and is shown here in 1959. It was similar in design to those built during the 1840s at various locations e.g. Culham, Stonehouse, Coates, etc., and, according to the illustration on page 8, Twyford also had a similar building. However, whilst it is believed to have been one of the original structures, the architects plans for Henley included a drawing for a slightly larger goods shed that was to have been built of brick and timber. The theory intimated on page 8 is, if anything, reinforced by the fact that 1857 was already late in time for this design, notwithstanding the possibility of an even later construction date. The main office at the north end of the building, illustrated above, was a very obvious addition of paler red brick built in 1899. The new office further extended a small lean-to which remained against the outside of the northern wall and served as a checker's office. The wooden platforms extending from either end of the building were probably added at the same time, and access between the covered platforms and the interior of the goods shed was improved by crudely enlarging the main railway entrances, the relevant brickwork being removed without disturbing the vital support of the stone lintels. The canopies were not provided until 1947 and were constructed using corrugated asbestos sheeting on railbuilt supports. A bin that was situated adjacent to the south end of the goods shed, behind the wooden platform, was reduced in size and removed to the opposite side of the access road, the apex of the fence being taken away to

accommodate it. The bin is said to have been an open enclosure built of blue brick with a small sliding hatch door in its base. The enclosure was used as a receptacle for the ashes from the station fires and sweepings from the yard, all of which was periodically loaded into wagons to be taken away.

Photos: Photoscript—Deddington & Author

A look back at the goods shed from alongside the back siding, again in 1959. The double rail-built loading gauge spanning both the loading bank and bay platform lines replaced the single wooden posted version, illustrated on page 41, during the 1920s. The small brick building at the end of the loading bank, just visible behind the bows of the boat, was used for station coal and possibly fodder for the small cattle pen. There was a reasonable cattle traffic at one time but the pen itself, which was situated on the south end of the loading bank, was rather modest in view of the size of the station.

With little industry in Henley as such, most of the goods were incoming and, predictably, mainly coal. When the railway first opened the town boasted two breweries, Messrs. Brakspears and Greys Brewery, but the latter closed in 1896. Brakspears continued to receive hops in quantity by rail and large hogsheads and cases of spirits as well as empty crates etc. Henley Saw Mills owned by Messers Ltd. received substantial quantities of timber and Messrs. Stuart Turner, builders of marine engines etc. also received various supplies. Other traffic received by rail included grain, fertilizer, livestock, animal foodstuffs, cable for Wessex Electricity Co., delivered on large cable drums, and a good deal of general merchandise. Outwards traffic had included considerable quantities of timber at one time, including occasional loads of pit props from Fawley Woods, livestock, general goods and completed or repaired engines from Stuart Turner's.

The GWR provided horse-drawn local collection and delivery services for goods and parcels. As many as six horses had been kept at Henley in the brick built stable, that was located to the west of the yard. This building was constructed in 1895 and can just be seen in the distance in the photograph on page 84. When the company later provided a motor lorry service, part of the stable was converted for use as a garage by the provision of large double doors and the removal of two of the stalls inside the building. In 1934 a 500-gallon petrol tank was also installed on the

eastern side of the stable 18″ below ground level. The new motor lorry was probably provided at about this time and covered the local area, but the horse-drawn services were retained to serve the town until after the Second World War.

Photoscript — Deddington

This corrugated iron warehouse was provided in 1936 for Messrs. Bibby's, agricultural feed merchants. The building was constructed to a standard GWR warehouse design of the time and was located at the very end of the long back siding. This new warehouse may well have replaced the grounded van body that stood to the south of the yard crane for a while during the 1930s. The corrugated iron shed on the right served as a lamp hut.

Author

The original 10 ton yard crane can just be discerned in the small picture above, but this was replaced about 1930 with the lighter crane illustrated here, which had a lifting capacity of only 6 tons. It has been suggested that the original crane was broken; if this was the case the more modern 6 ton version was evidently considered an adequate replacement.

Photoscript — Deddington

84

This photograph, taken between 1936 and 1939, shows the end of the long back siding, the new warehouse and the grounded van body to the south of the crane. The premises of Messer's, Henley Saw Mills, Dunlop's and Butler's backed on to the railway boundary alongside the back siding, out of the picture, which enabled deliveries to be unloaded and taken directly onto their own property. There were no coal pens in the yard as the other companies unloaded wagons directly onto carts and lorries and also stored the coal on their own premises so the yard was noticeably tidy and at one time regularly swept. Incidentally, the yard was metalled in 1928 by Messrs. Brown of Plymouth. Despite the GWR Company's provision of cast iron notices that warned against the dangerous practice of propping up the doors of wagons, for loading or unloading purposes, the practice nevertheless continued at least into the 1920s. The side doors of loaded coal wagons were carefully lowered onto suitable props and, after the initial spillage, the resulting platform was utilized by the coalmen while they continued to unload. The pick-up goods was formed up in the bay platform each morning which, because of its position alongside the simple goods yard, was ideal for the purpose. The white lines that were painted along the edges of the platform during the First World War were evidently not maintained. At this time, white lines were only required from October to March inclusive, but, although they were not required at all stations, Henley was not exempted.

Lens of Sutton

As already mentioned the main incoming traffic to Henley was undoubtedly coal for the needs of the town and local industry, including of course the Henley gas works. It is probably fair to say that Toomer, R & Co. Ltd. were the most prominent agents in the town, and this company in fact supplied the Henley Gas Company. The company's office, previously illustrated on page 75, was alongside the station and their yard was situated opposite and extended between Station Road and Friday Street. They were a large concern with other depots at Nine Elms, Windsor, Great Marlow and Reading and also ran their own fleet of wagons, examples of which are illustrated here. The wagons were provided by the Gloucester Carriage and Wagon Company Ltd. and painted plain black with white lettering, shaded red, although the shading was not applied to later wagons. Besides being coal factors, the company were also hay and straw merchants and importers of hay from abroad.

Other coal merchants included Messrs. Tayler & Co.; T. Smith & Co.; Oliver Hopkins, whose business was taken over after the death of the proprietor by Geo. Dunlop in November 1894; William Wakefield, whose business was taken over by Messrs. Holton about 1922; Butler; Pearcy; and Wilder who sold out to R. A. Turner in November 1945. Messrs. Geo. Dunlop and Butler ran their own wagons, the liveries of which are believed to have been black with white lettering. Incidentally, Butler's ran both Sentinel and Foden steam lorries that were frequently seen in the yard.

Holton's also owned about ten railway wagons which were again painted black but provided some variation in that their name 'HOLTONS' was painted with black lettering on a diagonal white band on the side of each vehicle, with 'Coal Factors Henley' and the wagon number appearing elsewhere on the side. The wagons, believed to have been supplied by the Wagon Repair Company, carried various numbers, the last vehicle purchased bearing the number 20. The accompanying photograph of one of these wagons is the only known view although one of the vehicles can just be seen in the photograph at the top of the facing page. The company's office was at No. 50 Queens Street behind which was a yard with coal pens, stable and hay loft. They kept about four horses which were grazed on the meadow behind what is now Sargeant's Garage but these were later replaced with motor lorries during the 1930s. The company operated until the Second World War when they lost their wagons to the Government and later sold out to Messrs. Toomer's in 1942. The picture at the foot of the facing page shows Cliff Ayres with one of Toomer's lorries (specially decorated) in the yard, probably just before the Second World War.

Photos: Gloucester Carriage & Wagon Co., Mr. & Mrs. V. Mellett, Geo. Bushell & Son, and J. Crawley

A similar view on 19th October, 1959, with No. 7029 *Clun Castle* at Henley on the 8.43 a.m. for Paddington. The enamel station nameboards were provided by British Railways during the early 1950s before which the station was only identified by the glass nameplates on the gas lamps as illustrated above. The glass plates were also replaced at the same time with slightly larger enamelled nameplates attached to the columns of the lamps.

R. J. Buckley

Looking south from the end of the main platform on 30th August 1947.

R. F. Roberts

0–6–0PT No. 5766 leaving Henley with the 5.40 p.m. to Twyford on 22nd September 1951.

M. W. Earley

Looking south on 1st August 1955, with the recently installed station nameboards at the end of the platforms. The centre pivot shunt arms bracketed to the bay starting signal were also fitted to the starting signals for platforms 1 and 2 but were replaced during the 1934 alterations with the route indicators illustrated.

J. N. Faulkner

This two-way wooden posted signal was understandably known to the staff as 'the Christmas tree'. It bore the 'up' main starting signal (to the left of main post) and the centre pivot 'up' main to 'down' sidings starting signal (to the right of the post) as shown in the illustration on the left. The opposite side of the signal, illustrated below, carried at the top the main to No. 1 platform inner home and beneath it the main to No. 1 platform calling on arm. Beneath the calling on arm were two centre pivot arms. The upper of these was the 'up' main to No. 3 platform starting signal, and the lower was the 'up' main to No. 2 platform starting signal. The No. 1 platform inner home signal applied to trains travelling 'down' the 'up' main. This will be more easily understood by reference to the signalling diagram on page 174. These two photographs were taken on 28th March 1954. The sleeper-built platelayers hut behind the signal box was used as the headquarters for the permanent way gang who also kept much of their stock there. The gang was made up of a ganger, sub ganger and four lengthmen, the ganger himself walking the length to Twyford every day. There had also been a corrugated iron lamp hut behind the box. This was provided in 1895 when the existing lamp room in the station building was converted to a cloakroom. The three water cranes at Henley were provided in 1905, the one illustrated below being situated on the 'up' side of the track near the signal box.   *Photos: Pat Moffatt and Author*

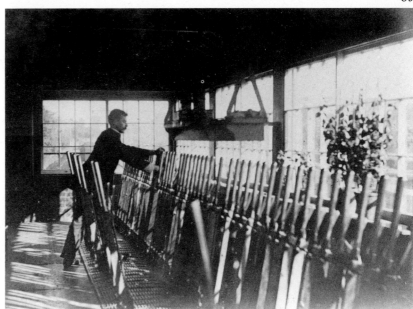

Signalman Ernest Paice inside the signal box c.1902.
G. W. Reeves, courtesy Miss S. Reeves

The extensive signal box, constructed of blue engineering brick with a slate roof, was brought into use in 1897. It was similar in design to Twyford West box and replaced a much smaller building with a 30 lever frame (signals 11, points 10, facing point locks 2 and 7 spares). The building is shown here on 28th March 1954, before the modifications to the sliding casements as shown on page 153. The doorway under the steps served a small store and the doorway at the opposite end had provided access to the base of the frame. Outside the building the signalmen maintained small gardens, the southernmost of which had a small goldfish pond. There was also a small hand pump not far from the base of the steps that was used to raise drinking water from a well.

Pat Moffatt

0–6–0PT No. 4649 leaving with a local train for Twyford on 7th September, 1947. The two vehicles in tow are converted 'toplight' and 'concertina' slip coaches respectively. The missing arm from the triple bracket intermediate home signal was removed during re-signalling in 1934 but the signal remained otherwise intact until 1956.   *J. H. Russell*

The extensive carriage sidings at Henley were used during the summer to hold excursion and other special trains, particularly during the intensive regatta service each year when whole trains were literally stockpiled in the sidings during the day awaiting their later return to Paddington. The easternmost sidings shown here were used for the overnight and weekend storage of the stock from the regular through trains to London, the remainder of the sidings being used during the winter for overflow storage of stock from the carriage depot at Old Oak Common. Empty stock usually arrived for storage in September each year and remained there until the following Whitsun. However, some of the stock was often collected on Christmas Eve and Good Friday and was away for two or three days for use on the Christmas and Easter services. Carriage cleaners were sent from Reading or Southall before coaches were required but there were also carriage cleaners at Henley and the sidings were equipped with hydrants for replenishing water supplies on the vehicles and for washing and cleaning purposes. Before the Second World War there had been two women carriage cleaners but these posts were resumed by male staff later. Empty stock trains were often taken straight from or to services at Paddington and a variety of motive power was provided for these stock movements. Two of the branch coaches are featured in the foreground of this rural scene alongside the sidings.   *HMRS*

A 1950s view of the sidings on either side of the double track as seen from Mill Lane bridge on a summer's evening about 1960. The sidings themselves were numbered 1 to 7 from left to right. Whilst No. 1 served as a headshunt for the yard and was consequently kept clear, Nos. 2-4 were used for stock storage, as was No. 5 (latterly) on the opposite side of the running lines. Nos. 6 and 7, as already mentioned, were used for the London through trains. This numbering sequence was rather unusual as it had been standard GW practice to number the sidings away from each running line. However, this system was altered in 1956 when the sidings were renumbered as part of the re-signalling and the headshunt on the left of the picture, for instance, became 'down' siding No. 4. For reasons of economy, the sidings had originally been laid with flat bottomed rail which in 1947 remained on 'down' sidings Nos. 1-3 and 'up' siding No. 1, but the relaying at the station that year is thought to have included the 'down' sidings. The replacement track was laid with concrete blocks and tiebars which were introduced in 1940 for use on sidings in order to conserve timber supplies from abroad. The timber shortage arose from shipping restrictions during the war and the limited supplies available were needed for use on the main lines. As this photograph shows, what had become 'up' siding No. 1 retained the flat bottomed rail until it was shortened in 1961.

B. W. Hughes

The end of the sidings and the bridge that carried Mill Lane over the railway. The bridge, constructed of blue engineering brick with a wrought iron girder span, was built in 1897 to replace a level crossing that had been situated just to the south. The small brick built hut was the second P.W. hut out of Henley and used for the storage of fishplates, bolts, rail jacks, etc.   *Author*

Brian Wright

'Hall' class 4—6—0 No. 4951 *Pendeford Hall* drifting past Mill Lane signal box on its way into Henley with a five coach train from Paddington during the 1950s. This picture was taken looking south from Mill Lane bridge and shows the row of tall elm trees in the distance that indicated the location of Sheephouse Farm crossing, the whistle board for which can be seen behind the loco.

Looking south from the road approach to Mill Lane bridge, showing the rear of the signal box. *Author*

Mill Lane signal box was built in 1896 alongside the level crossing that once existed here. The roadway had originally run between the crossing keeper's house and the signal box, and even today its course is still apparent at either end of the approaches to the bridge. The electric train staff system of regulating trains over the single line was introduced on the branch in 1894. When the signal box was opened it became another block post. The signal box remained after the doubling and subsequent replacement of the level crossing to provide an additional block section which increased the line's capacity during the heavy regatta traffic. Certainly during the last years of its short working life it was only opened for the duration of the regatta each year and manned by a relief signalman from Reading. The signals controlled by this box remained after its closure in 1919 with 'out of use' crosses attached to their arms, illustrated on page 37, and were not removed until 1924 when a trailing crossover just north of the bridge was also taken out. The building itself survived into the late 1960s, leased by one of the line's former staff for use as a greenhouse, and the crossing keeper's house, which is illustrated on page 40, still survives as a private residence although now doubled in size. *Author*

SHIPLAKE

A distant view of Shiplake station as seen across the meadows from Mill Road at the beginning of the century. *Lens of Sutton*

Station Road, looking towards the station and river. The station house on the right and the lay-by alongside were built in 1897 during the doubling. The lay-by was enclosed with timber fencing and used as a car park in later years.

British Railways

Looking towards the Thames from the station footbridge at the beginning of the century. The riverside meadows were part of the Bolney Court Estate, but gradually disappeared as the land was sold for property development. This commenced in 1900 with the sale of fourteen riverside plots near Bolney Road and over the next twenty years most of Lower Shiplake was developed around the station.

Courtesy C. B. Savory

This view, also taken from the station footbridge, shows Station Road c.1914.

Courtesy John Crocker

Looking south from the level crossing along the 'down' line towards Twyford about 1960. When the line was doubled the widened platform was divided into two separate ramps at this end, separated by a loading bay into which road vehicles could be backed, doubtless for milk traffic.   *Lens of Sutton*

A closer view of the small goods shed. When originally built it was constructed entirely of timber with a slate roof and a sliding door. The brick plinth was a later addition and probably the reason that the sliding door was modified to run inside the building.   *A. Attewell*

Looking south from the footbridge over the station in 1919. Prior to the erection of the ticket barrier at Henley, tickets were examined at Shiplake and often caused considerable delay. The wooden hut at the far end of the platform was a temporary building provided each year for the regatta. This was used by a team of some four or five ticket inspectors posted to Shiplake to cope with the exceptional passenger traffic bound for Henley.   *L. & G.R.P.*

Still looking south, this time over the 'up' running line in 1964. The corrugated iron shed in the foreground stood at the foot of the steps from the footbridge. It was provided during the early years of the century to serve as a parcels office and necessitated the removal of the station nameboard, illustrated on page 94, to the opposite end of the main building.   *A. E. Smith*

The level crossing, seen from the footbridge during the late 1950s, dates from 1897 and replaced what appears to have been a simple occupation crossing over the single line. The gates were manually operated although they would close by gravity when they were not latched to the posts at the foot of the platform. If allowed to return unchecked the heavy timber gates gathered considerable momentum before closing across the road with a resounding crash that became a frequent and familiar sound to residents in the local neighbourhood. The wicket gates alongside were kept locked and only used for the passage of heavy luggage, milk, etc. Passengers were requested to cross the line by the footbridge that maintained a public right of way over the railway and provided access to the island platform. The crossing gates were locked by a lever in the signal box which had to be in the normal position before the signals protecting the crossing could be cleared. The corrugated iron shed between the tracks served as a lamp room and had originally been sited at the rear of the single sided platform at the south end of the new building. The station was originally oil lit but in 1913 the lighting was converted for petrol air gas. The apparatus was housed in the lamp hut where the gas was collected over a water tank. During the winter bunsen burners were apparently used to prevent the water from freezing. The system is said to have proved troublesome and was eventually replaced by electric lighting. When the new signal box was provided in 1961 the lamp shed was moved over to the far side of the crossing and survived there into the 1970s. The notice on the 'down' side crossing gate, shown in the inset, had read 'Take care — these self locking gates close quickly'.   *A. Attewell*

The two sidings in the small goods yard were known as 'front' and 'back' and could only be serviced from the 'down' direction. On this occasion, during the 1950s, the yard was deserted but it was very busy at one time and had generally been full. Outgoing traffic handled there included hay, straw, corn and pit props and other timber from Coppice Farm. The local coal merchant, a Mr. Quaint, had a coal office in the yard and stored his coal along the back siding. He also apparently owned two or three railway wagons which are said to have borne his name. Mr. Quaint had a farm at Binfield Heath and also ran a carriers service. He had two horse-drawn carts and kept his horses in the stables which can be seen behind the yard. The service was operated until the 1930s when the railway took over the local deliveries. Messrs. Dunlop succeeded Mr. Quaint as local coal merchant at Shiplake. The camping coach was first provided at the station some time after the one at Wargrave. The vehicle here was succeeded by an eight-wheeled clerestory coach and at one time Sir Charles J. Hambro, Chairman of the GWR from 1940-45, stayed here in one of the coaches.

A. Attewell

A 3½ ton yard crane was provided in 1893 but by 1904 had been replaced with the smaller 1½ ton version illustrated here.

Pat Moffatt

This final view from the footbridge shows how the 'down' running line resumed its position alongside the 'up' line as it headed away from the north of the station towards Henley. The sleeper-built hut featured in both these views, by the loading gauge, was a platelayers cabin. The photograph was taken on 15th June, 1958.

Pat Moffatt

A closer view of the footpath that can be seen crossing the line in the previous photograph and still maintains a public right of way over it.

A. Attewell

Looking south from the footpath towards the station on 29th June, 1958.   *Pat Moffatt*

Top left This signal box housing a 17 lever frame, was built in 1897 during the layout revisions carried out for the doubling. Sadly no details are known of the previous building, which was situated on the passenger platform.

A. Attewell

Top right The interior of the signal box with Taffy Hopkins behind the 17 lever frame on 14th January, 1961. In quieter moments the signalman often helped out in the yard with the roping and sheeting of wagons.

Pat Moffatt

The signal box was a contemporary of the Mill Lane box but constructed of red and blue bricks with a slate roof. It is shown here in GWR colours on 5th August 1953, complete with a lucky horseshoe over the little porch. During the late 1950s the chimney stack was removed and replaced with a stovepipe.

Pat Moffatt

The station building was constructed of red brick with a blue brick plinth and reveals. When first built in 1892 it was fitted with a small canopy which projected over the single platform that existed at the time. It is shown in this condition in the drawing on page 164. Access to the platform was via a ramp at each end, the rear of the platform being fenced with timber palings and backing onto a meadow. The doorways were therefore concentrated along the platform side and in each end of the structure, with windows provided at the rear. When the branch was doubled shortly afterwards, the new 'down' line was routed behind the original station. The platform was extended across to serve the new line, becoming an island platform, and the canopy of the building was extended to overhang all the way around the structure. The utilization of the existing new station in the doubling of the line obviously made economic sense and, although the overall layout that evolved as a direct result of the modifications was rather unusual, it was nevertheless quite attractive.

The accommodation of the building consisted of, from left to right, gentlemen's lavatory, station office, waiting room and booking hall, with the usual ticket window, ladies waiting room and lavatory and at the far end a store used for cleaning equipment etc., served by a door in the end of the building.

A. Attewell

Another picture of Bert Broad *(right)* as a young lad porter at Shiplake about 1920.

Courtesy Gary Broad

The station gardens both on and opposite the platform were well cared for and lent a welcoming air to the station. One of the flowerbeds even included a small goldfish pond. This photograph was taken on 5th August, 1953.
Pat Moffatt

This contemporary photograph taken on 8th August 1953, shows the wooden posted 'down' home signal that stood just south of the foot of the platform. In 1956 both this and the wooden posted 'up' starting signal were replaced with the tubular steel posted signals shown opposite. It is also evident that the opportunity was also taken at this time to re-site the 'down' home signal further south so that it was not obscured by the trees that had since developed. *Pat Moffatt*

The footpath flanking either side of the railway at this point had crossed the railway approximately in line with the end of the iron railings on the left. However, the 500 ft extension of the original platform in 1892 necessitated a diversion of the path to cross the line further south. In 1897 the footpath was diverted again to clear a further 100 ft extension of the platform during the doubling.

Lens of Sutton

Looking south from the end of the station platform towards Wargrave on 29th June, 1958.

Pat Moffatt

1881 track plan

S.P.

To Henley

S.P.

P.W. Hut

Pond

To

S.P

Level Crossing

Lashbrook Hotel

Office

Level Crossing

Shiplake Signal Box

Parcels

Parcels

Station Building

Nameboard

S.P.

Disc

To Henley

Disc

Disc

Disc

Loading Gauge

1½ Ton Crane

Coal

Oil

Oil

L.P.

L.P.

S.P.

Station Master's House

33

Station Building

Parcels Shed

Cycle Shed

S.P.

Nameboard

Footbridge

To Shiplake

Wargrave Viaduct

Waiting Room

S.P.

P L

L.P.

L.P.

P L

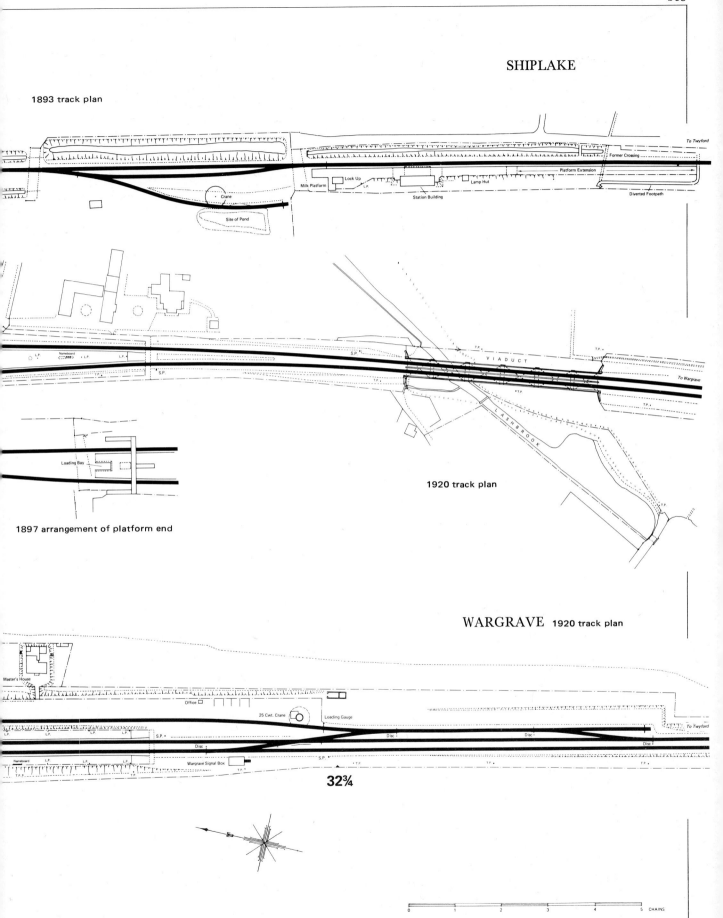

SHIPLAKE

1893 track plan

To Twyford
Former Crossing
Platform Extension
Diverted Footpath
Milk Platform
Lock Up
Station Building
Lamp Hut
Crane
Site of Pond

1920 track plan

VIADUCT
To Wargrave
LASHBROOK

1897 arrangement of platform end

Loading Bay
Nameboard

WARGRAVE 1920 track plan

Master's House
Office
25 Cwt. Crane
Loading Gauge
To Twyford
Wargrave Signal Box
Nameboard

32¾

0 1 2 3 4 5 CHAINS

WARGRAVE

Looking north towards Henley from the 'down' platform at Wargrave station during the late 1950s. The station buildings were constructed of red brick with blue brick plinths and slate roofs, but, unlike the earlier building at Shiplake, the moulded reveals to the doors and windows were not picked out with blue brick. The main building on the opposite platform was at first supplemented by a single corrugated iron shed alongside, the second being provided at the end of 1901. The nearest to the camera served as a bicycle shed and the one next to the building was used as a parcels office. The provision of a corrugated asbestos bicycle shed, which can just be seen on the 'up' platform at the base of the footbridge,

necessitated the removal of the station nameboard from this site to the opposite end of the station building as shown. The station was gas lit, electricity not being provided until about 1970, long after the 'down' building and platform had gone. Staff took their own tea with them as there was no drinking water at the site until 1946, before which time water was drawn from a well by a small hand pump situated in the gentlemen's lavatory, and stored in a 200 gallon tank in the roof of the building. The station had been staffed with a station master, two porter-signalmen and two lad porters.

Lens of Sutton

The station was approached from the village by a long and straight purpose built road which opened out through wooden entrance gates into a forecourt alongside the main station building. There were no doors in the rear of the main building and this gate in the iron railings was the only official means of access to the platforms. The mail from the village was brought to the station each evening in a hand cart pushed by one of the postmen, and on arrival the cart was wheeled straight onto the platform to meet the train. In bad weather or fading light a red lamp was hung on this vehicle which on one occasion was unknowingly left shining straight down the track. This caused the branch train to brake and approach the station with extreme caution, and, not surprisingly, when the source of the red light became apparent, the driver was rather angry!

A. Attewell

Milk, collected each day by the 3.50 p.m. mixed train from Henley, was loaded from the main platform. The old 17 gallon churns were tall and heavy to handle but the porters could skilfully spin them along the platform with one under each hand. The accommodation of the main building consisted of a station office on the left, followed by a waiting room, served by a small ticket window from the office, ladies waiting room and lavatory, and at the far end of the building, the gentlemen's lavatories, the timber screen alongside the entrance to which bore the usual row of red painted fire buckets. This photograph was taken on 19th July 1958, after the removal of the signalling and shows the security bars that were fitted to the station offices on the branch during the mid-1950s.   *Pat Moffatt*

Diesel railcar No. 1 alongside the 'up' platform at Wargrave during the early 1950s.   *Lens of Sutton*

This photograph of the 'down' side steps of the station footbridge also illustrates an example of one of the shades fitted to strategically positioned lamps which remained in use during the Second World War. The small gate at the foot of the steps served a private house formerly called 'Bon Accord'. A path led down a flight of steps into the garden of the property and had proved quite invaluable to residents when the river was in flood. At these times the road crossed by Wargrave viaduct was completely under water and this path apparently became the only means of access.

Photoscript — Deddington

The bicycle shed was provided in 1946 at a cost of £110. It is shown here after the removal of the footbridge. *D. J. Hyde*

The small waiting room was the only building on the 'down' platform. It was provided with a small fireplace and fitted with continuous wooden benches fixed to the walls inside. The embankment fell away steeply at the rear of the building, exposing the brick arch foundations.

A. Attewell

Looking south over the station during 1921 showing the trees that skirted the eastern boundary alongside the goods yard and the open farmland to the west. *L. & G.R.P.*

Another view of railcar No. 1 at Wargrave, this time on its way to Henley during the early 1950s. *Lens of Sutton*

The station forecourt during the early 1950s, showing the rear of the main building and the entrance gate beyond. A horse-drawn carriers service was run by the White Hart Hotel in the village who later provided a motor taxi service with their Napier taxi. Fred Brown, who succeeded the hotel as a local carrier, also ran a Brougham, William Butler ran a taxi service with a Talbot Darracq and about 1939 Mr. Bird and his son were also running taxis.

A. Attewell

When George Tranter was the station master for both Wargrave and Shiplake he lived in the station house at Wargrave and the house at Shiplake was let to signalman Eddie Goodey and his wife and another signalman, Jack Stimpson. The station house at Wargrave was built in 1902 and constructed of red brick with a slate roof. It was located alongside the goods yard and because the station master objected to wagons being unloaded in front of his home, vehicles were generally kept as far 'up' the siding as possible. Wet fish deliveries arrived on the early train each morning for W. Messam, the local fishmonger. They were carried in the guard's van but the empty boxes were stacked on the edge of the yard, just past the station house (!) and left to accumulate until justifying a wagon load. The end loading bank had been used to load the occasional car but could not be used at all after the provision of the camping coach that was stabled at the end of the yard siding.

Pat Moffatt

A camp coach was provided at Wargrave by 1936 at which time the vehicle provided had a 4-berth capacity and was oil lit. A larger 6-berth vehicle that later replaced this was equipped with Calor gas and there had once been two such vehicles here at the same time. This beautifully posed publicity photograph was taken on the 12th June 1957, probably from the station house.

British Railways

Looking south towards Twyford from the foot of the station platform on 13th July, 1954, showing part of the goods yard and the corrugated iron lamp shed. Plans were drawn in 1932 for a private siding that was proposed at Wargrave for Messrs. H. G. Smith. Briefly, the proposals included a loop alongside the 'down' running line, with trailing connections from both the 'up' and 'down' lines, extending from the Wargrave Lane overbridge, which can be seen in the distance, to the signal box. This would have served a private siding which was to diverge westwards from behind the signal box, on a falling gradient, to cross the River Loddon. However, nothing came of this scheme and no further details have been discovered.
Pat Moffatt

The signal box was constructed of red brick with blue brick plinth, quoins, reveals and lintels. It is believed to have opened on 2nd January 1901, and to have been manned at first by a full time signalman. However, it was closed at about the time of the Great War and thereafter only switched in as required to deal with the branch goods, for which purpose it was manned by a porter-signalman. With the heavy traffic on the branch, the signal box was used during the regatta each year, when it was switched in from about 6.00 p.m. to about 8.30 p.m. to provide an extra block section, to increase the line's capacity, and manned by a relief signalman from Reading. On the Saturday of the event it apparently remained open until about 1.30 a.m. the following morning. When the box was switched out all the signals were left in the clear position as seen above. The signalling consisted of distant, home and starting signals for each direction with an advanced starting signal in the 'up' direction only, the yard access being signalled with ground discs. The signal box shown here on 13th July 1954 was completely closed on 3rd October that year. The trailing crossover from the 'down' line was subsequently removed and a single lever ground frame, released from Shiplake box, was provided to control the trailing connection to the yard from the 'up' line. The top of the building was removed in 1957/8, the base being provided with a flat roof and retained as a platelayers cabin.

Pat Moffatt

Looking back over the station and yard on 13th July 1954.

Pat Moffatt

Messrs. Richard Webster & Sons Ltd of Maidenhead were local coal merchants at Wargrave and also had other depots at Bourne End, Taplow and Burnham. The company had their own wagons which were painted a basic colour of chocolate brown with a diagonal red band and white lettering shaded black. Another local coal merchant was a Mr. Tuck whose coal was supplied by Messrs. Talbot's of Reading and arrived in that company's wagons. Mr. Tuck was later succeeded by a Mr. Franklin. The privately owned coal pens in the yard were constructed from old sleepers but the station coal was kept in the brick-built enclosure at the edge of the yard just south of the crane.

Gloucester Railway Carriage and Wagon Co. Ltd.

A 6 ton yard crane had originally been provided at Wargrave, but traffic evidently failed to reach expectations and by 1925 it was replaced by a smaller 25 cwt machine. This was short-lived as it was pulled over in a shunting mishap in 1930 when the hook became caught on a sheet rail of a moving wagon. It was replaced by a new 3 ton version supplied by Messrs. Holt & Willett and illustrated here. However, the new crane saw little use as there was not much outward traffic and, apart from coal, incoming traffic mainly included potatoes and general merchandise for the village. There was no weighbridge at Wargrave so loads that required checking were weighed at Twyford. There had been a small platelayers hut just south of the loading gauge, which was also used to store salt.

Author

TWYFORD

An unidentified 'Saint' class 4—6—0 speeding through Twyford in 1912 with a fast train to Paddington. The Henley branch loco can just be seen over the far side of the station in the branch bay.   *British Railways*

The original station at Twyford was completely swept away when the station was rebuilt in connection with the quadrupling of the main line. The new station is seen here from the road bridge looking west towards Reading in 1919. One of the familiar corrugated iron 'pagoda' sheds was provided on the 'up' relief platform the following year for use as a bicycle shed.   *L. & G.R.P.*

No. 6027 *King Richard I* heading through Twyford on the 'down' main line with an express from Paddington on 16th August, 1947.

H. C. Casserley

Looking towards Paddington from Platform 4 about 1958. The enamelled station nameboards had already replaced those shown in previous views at this time and the gas lamps were replaced with concrete post electric lamps in 1959.

Lens of Sutton

This photograph was again taken from the road bridge in 1919, but this time looking east towards Paddington. The running crossovers between the 'main' and 'relief' lines are well illustrated here and were used by many of the through trains between Henley and Paddington. The 'down' relief refuge siding can just be seen beyond Twyford East Signal Box and through the years was used to hold various local trains or stock for the Henley branch.

L. & G.R.P.

No. 6936 *Breccles Hall* crossing over from the main to the relief line as it enters Twyford station with a train from Paddington in July 1959. This was the path taken by most of the through trains for Henley.

J. A. Fleming

An aerial view of Twyford station on 14th September 1929, clearly showing the junction for the Henley branch and the location of the bay platform. The siding diverging from the branch run round loop served a small coal yard in which Messrs. Toomer's had an office. This remained as what could be described as a 'hang-over' from the original goods yard and was officially known as the gasworks siding. Coincidentally, gas tank wagons or 'Cordons' that replenished the gas cylinders on the branch coaches, were also stabled there. Twyford Gas Works was built about 1858, but was greatly developed about 1885 when the local streets were lighted and a new retort and gas holder provided. A gas main was laid to Wargrave in 1896 but Twyford, Wargrave and Henley were later supplied by the Yorktown and Camberley Gas Co. in 1931. The gas works at Twyford, illustrated in the lower part of this photograph, was subsequently demolished in 1933. A new weighing machine was provided in 1930 for the weighbridge at Twyford, the building of which is still situated alongside the road just outside the entrance to the small yard. The corrugated iron shed nearest to the cattle pens was used for the storage of barrels of oil whilst the other was used by the lampman. This photograph also shows the trailing connection to the mill siding that joined the 'up' line of the branch just short of the branch's own connection with the 'up' relief line. The station master's house on the edge of the forecourt was built in 1900. *Aerofilms*

An early postcard view of the station c.1905 with Twyford West Signal Box in the foreground and the Henley branch train waiting in the branch bay on the left.

M. E. J. Deane

The Royal Station Hotel just opposite the station. The bar of this establishment was favoured by a number of the railway staff!

Courtesy Gary Broad

Looking away from the railway along Station Road.

Courtesy Gary Broad

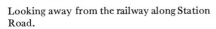

Looking along the branch bay towards the buffer stops during the early 1950s. The headshunt beyond the engine release crossover was large enough to accommodate 'Hall' class 4—6—0s which sometimes worked into the bay in the morning with the first train from Henley. The buffer stops at the end of the bay were enclosed with wooden gates and served for end loading purposes. Until the late 1960s passengers from Henley had to go outside the station in order to gain access to the footbridge, but this arrangement was later improved by the provision of an entirely new staircase to give direct access to the bridge from the branch bay. Before this, the area currently occupied by these steps was used to stable the numerous four-wheeled platform trolleys.

A. Attewell

The cattle pens opposite the branch platform saw considerable use as there was a good deal of cattle traffic. Cattle wagons were kept at the end of the siding and moved, with the aid of a pinch bar, alongside the pens as required.

A. Attewell

Looking along the branch bay from the rear of the cab of the branch loco No. 9758, on 5th August, 1935, with the lamp iron on the top of the bunker unfortunately prominent in the foreground.

Jack Crawley

The new goods yard dated from 1892 and was isolated in a triangular plot between the main line, the branch curve and the River Loddon. A narrow and steeply inclined service road, leading from a minor lane that ran under the railway, was the sole means of access. The accommodation of the new goods yard was still somewhat cramped and the yard could only be shunted when the 'up' relief line was clear between trains as there was no room for a headshunt. The substantial goods shed, which was similar to the one at Maidenhead, was also built in 1892 and replaced the original one shown on page 160. The siding that served Twyford mill can just be seen diverging to the left on the outside of the branch curve.

Once inside the gate, on the mill premises, the siding ran alongside the mill before turning sharply to terminate alongside the High Street. There had also been a short spur opposite the mill itself. The mill was bought by Berks Bucks & Oxon Farmers in 1927 and subsequently used for compounding livestock foodstuffs. In 1934 the siding was altered to provide a storage loop, capable of holding 9 wagons, which converged again alongside the end of the building. Some excavation had been necessary to accommodate the new arrangement, the siding was moved some 4-5 feet away from the mill and a new hoist provided on the side of the building for loading purposes. Locomotives were only allowed into the siding as far as the stop board that was located just before the new hoist and because of the exceptionally sharp curve at the end of the siding, wagons had to be pushed round by hand. The mill itself is illustrated on page 21 shortly after construction. This aerial photograph was taken on 14th September 1929.

Aerofilms

The rear of Twyford West Signal Box about 1960. As the views on these pages show, the 'down' relief platform extended beyond those serving the main lines. This photograph shows the new fencing that had recently replaced the timber palings, featured above, which extended along the rear of the platform. The wooden shed alongside the signal box was used by the signal lineman.

Cecil J. Blay

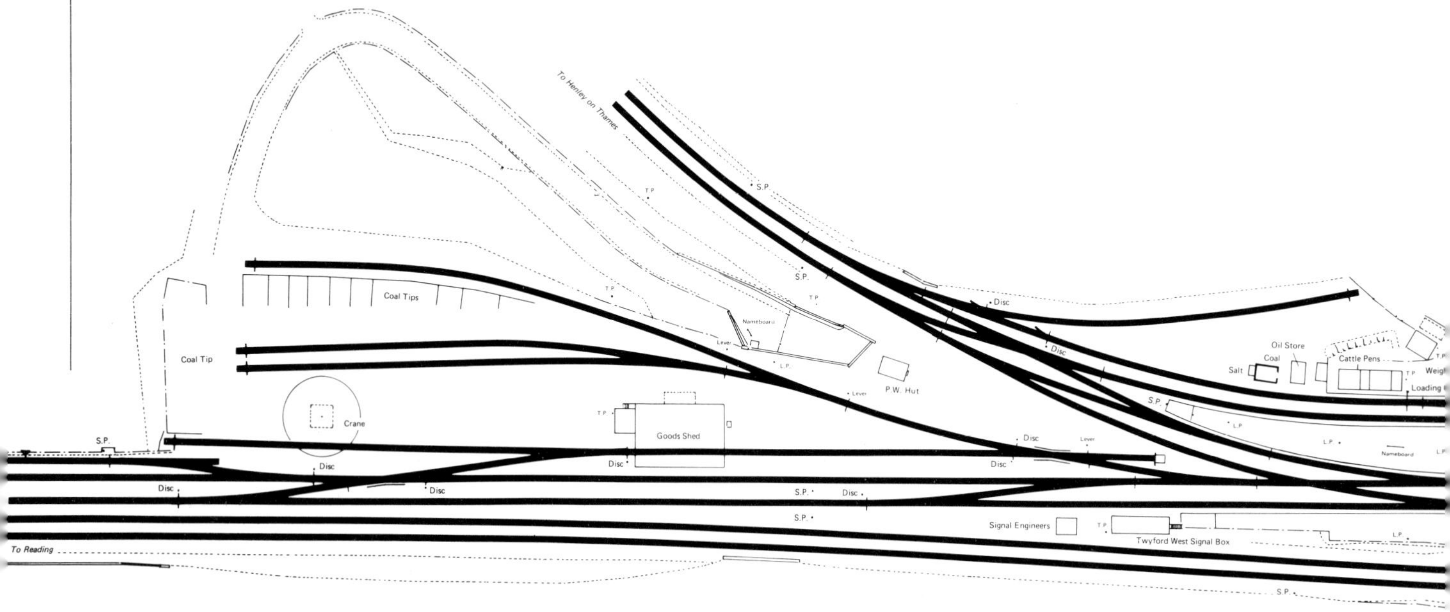

To Henley on Thames

S.P.

Coal Tips

Coal Tip

T.P.

T.P.

Disc

Oil Store

Coal

Cattle Pens

Weigh

Salt

Nameboard

Loading

Lever

P.W. Hut

Disc

Crane

S.P.

T.P.

Goods Shed

Disc

Lever

Disc

S.P.

L.F.

Nameboard

S.P.

Disc

Disc

Disc

Disc

Lever

Disc

S.P.

Disc

To Reading

S.P.

Signal Engineers

T.P.

Twyford West Signal Box

L.F.

S.P.

A

A

TWYFORD MILL SIDING

To Henley

S.B.

Gate

RISING GRADIENT 1 IN 98

Signal Box 480 yds from main box

DAVIS' MILL

To Henley

Office

Office

Gate

ENGINES MUST NOT PASS THIS BOARD

PUBLIC ROAD

Hoist

Oil Tank

MILL

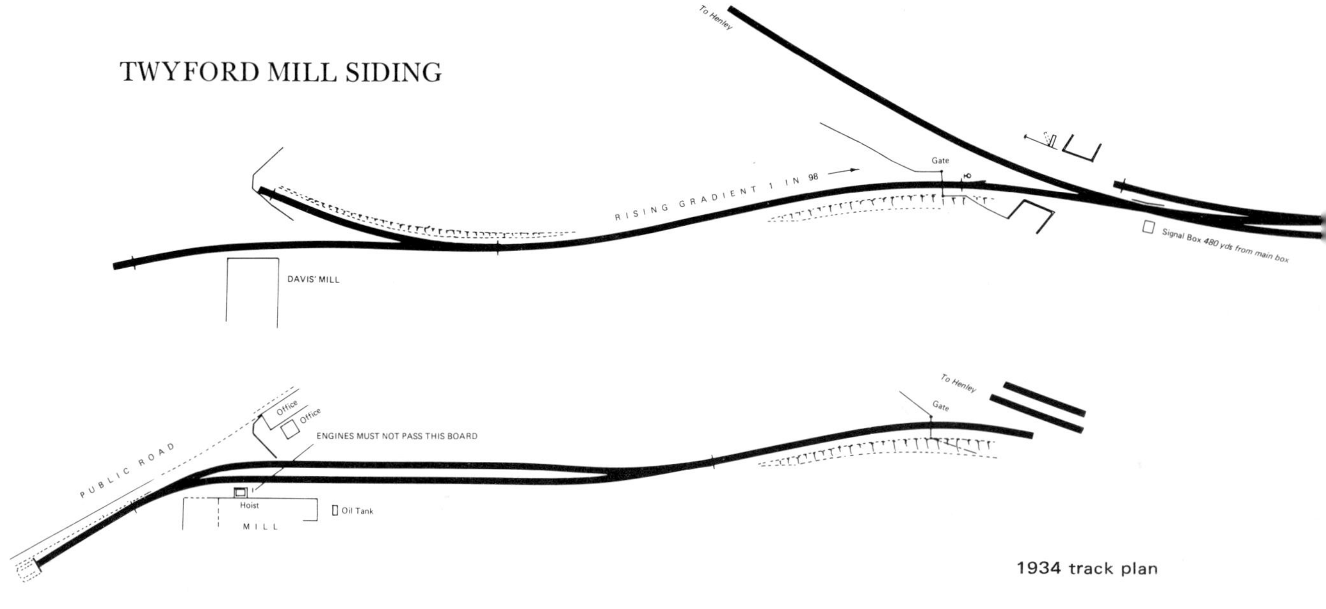

1934 track plan

TWYFORD c.1950 track plan

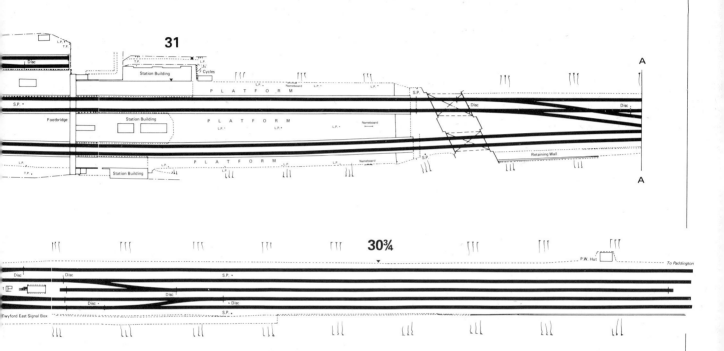

31

A

Disc

S.P.

Disc

Disc

Footbridge

Station Building

Station Building

P L A T F O R M

Nameboard

P L A T F O R M

Nameboard

Retaining Wall

P L A T F O R M

Nameboard

Station Building

A

30¾

P.W. Hut

To Paddington

Disc

Disc

S.P.

Disc

Disc

Twyford East Signal Box

S.P.

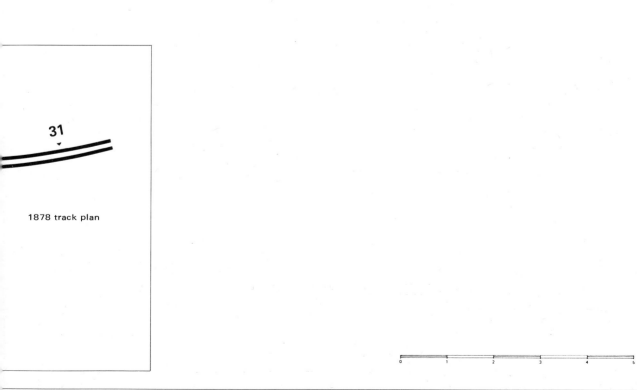

31

1878 track plan

0   1   2   3   4   5   CHAINS

HENLEY-ON-THAMES BRANCH.

DOUBLE LINE.

Trains booked to run into the Bay Line at Twyford must not convey more than six eight-wheel coaches containing passengers when worked by a Tank Engine, and not more than five when worked by a Tender Engine.

WEEK DAYS.

Distance	DOWN TRAINS. STATIONS.	Ruling gradient 1 in	Point to point times	Allow for stop.	Allow for start.																													

(Columns marked: MX B, V B K, P B C, G Eng. Van Q, numerous B Pas. / Auto Pas. / Thro Pas. / Pass. columns, SO B, SXSO B, etc.)

M.C.	Station	Ruling	Mins	Mins	Mins	A.M.	A.M.	A.M.	A.M.	A.M.	A.M.	A.M.	A.M.	A.M.	A.M.	A.M.	A.M.	A.M.	A.M.	A.M.	A.M.	A.M.	P.M.	P.M.	P.M.	P.M.	P.M.	P.M.	P.M.	P.M.	P.M.	P.M.	P.M.
—	Twyford ..	—	—		1	12 38	1 16	5 48	6 37	6‖48	7 33	7 55	8 16	9 20	10 26	10 42	11 3	11 12	12 15	1235	1 6	1 19	1 37	2 2	2 25	2 42	3 5	3 12	3 56	4 13	4 55	5 10	5 31
1 66	Wargrave ..	64 F	4	1	1	12 43	1 20	6 15	6 42		7 37	8 1	8 20	9 24	10 6	10 46	11 7	11 17	12 19	1239	1 11	1 23	1 41	2 7	2 29	2 46	3 9	3 16	4 0	4 35	4 59	5 14	5 36
2 59	Shiplake .. {	101 R	3	1	1	1245½	1 22	6 20	6 44		7 39	8 3	8 22	9 26	10 8	10 48	11 9	11½4	12 21	1241	1 14	1 25	1 43	2 9	2 31	2 48	5 11	3 18	4 2	4 37	5 1	5 16	5 38
4 48	Henley	L	5	1	1	12 51	1 28	6 39	6 52	7‖ 0	7 45	8 9	8 28	9 32	10 14	10 54	11 16	11 25	12 27	1247	1 20	1 31	1 49	2 15	2 38	2 54	3 17	3 25	4 8	4 43	5 7	5 22	5 44

WEEK DAYS—cont. / **SUNDAYS.**

(DOWN TRAINS. STATIONS: Twyford, Wargrave, Shiplake, Henley — continuation and Sunday columns of Pas./Thro Pas./Auto Pas. times.)

Notes (Down)

J Guard to collect or issue Wargrave tickets.   **P** With Newspapers and Parcels traffic.   **Q** From Reading, for 8.18 a.m. Henley.   **T** Tickets to be collected at Henley.
V Wargrave arrive 5.5½ a.m.   **W** Commences May 25th, 1930.   **Y** Not after May 18th, 1930.   **Z** On Saturdays through passenger from Paddington, Twyford depart 2.49 p.m.,
Henley arrive 3.2 p.m.   **§** Worked by Auto Car on Saturdays.   * To connect for newspapers off 6.25 a.m. Auto ex Reading, but Branch Trip must not be kept later than 6.42 a.m.

Farm Occupation Crossings between Shiplake and Henley.—Drivers must keep a sharp look-out and sound their whistles when approaching the two Farm Occupation Crossings between Shiplake and Henley.

HENLEY-ON-THAMES BRANCH.

DOUBLE LINE.

Trains booked to run into the Bay Line at Twyford must not convey more than six eight-wheel coaches containing passengers when worked by a Tank Engine, and not more than five when worked by a Tender Engine.

WEEK DAYS.

UP TRAINS. STATIONS.	Ruling gradient 1 in	Point to point times	Allow for stop.	Allow for start.																									

Station	Ruling	Mins	Mins	Mins	A.M.	A.M.	A.M.	A.M.	A.M.	A.M.	A.M.	A.M.	A.M.	A.M.	A.M.	A.M.	A.M.	A.M.	P.M.	P.M.	P.M.	P.M.	P.M.	P.M.	P.M.	P.M.	P.M.	P.M.
Henley ..	—	—		1	12 55	1†40	7 8	7 27	7 55	8 18	8 50	9 15	9‖26	10 0	10 45	11 10	11 32	11 45	12 12	12 55	1 16	1 33	1 58	2 20	3 5	3 30	3 50	4 25	5 27	5‖52	5 48	5 58
Shiplake {	L	5	1	1	12 58	—	7 11	7 30	7 58	8 21	8 53	9 18		10 3	10 48	11 14	11 35	**CR**	12 16	12 59	1 20	1 37	2 2	2 24	3 9	3 33	3 54	4 28	5 30		5 52	6 2
Wargrave {	70 R	3	1	1	1 3‖	1V51	7 16	7 35	8 3	8 26	8 59	9 23		10 8	10 53	11 18	11 40	**CR**	12 20	1 3	1 24	1 41	2 6	2 28	3 13	3 38	3 58	4 33	5 35	—	5 56	6 6
Twyford ..	64 R	5	1	1	1 8‖	1 8‖47	7 20	7 39	8 7	8 30	9 3	9 27	9‖35	10 12	10 57	11 22	11 45	12 10	12 24	1 7	1 28	1 45	2 10	2 33	3 17	3 42	4 7	4 37	5 40	5‖44	6 0	6 10

WEEK DAYS. / **SUNDAYS.**

(UP TRAINS continuation and Sunday columns — Henley, Shiplake, Wargrave, Twyford.)

Notes (Up)

J Guard to collect or issue Wargrave Tickets.   **P** Not after May 18th, 1930.   **Q** Runs one minute later on Saturdays.   **R** Commences June 2nd, 1930.   **V** Guard to extinguish lights and close Wargrave Station.   **W** Commences May 25th, 1930.   **Y** Branch train until May 18th, 1930. Through train to Paddington commencing May 25th, 1930.
§ Forms 3.25 p.m. Twyford to Reading on Saturdays.

Farm Occupation Crossings between Shiplake and Henley.—Drivers must keep a sharp look-out and sound their whistles when approaching the two Farm Occupation Crossings between Shiplake and Henley.

CHAPTER SIX

OPERATION

OPERATION of the Henley branch was very complex for a comparatively simple line and furthermore varied through the years. The following chapter is an attempt to outline a typical weekday from the 1929 timetable by piecing together evidence gathered from various sources including members of the crews involved. Unless hitherto undiscovered records are found to exist, many of the permutations of the workings over the years will probably simply remain as unexplained entries on the working timetables. However, whilst much of the working of the branch coaching stock remains a mystery, the following notes should at least present some idea of the operations involved. At the time described there were two drivers and two firemen based at Henley and an overnight shedman who travelled in from Reading each evening. The branch locomotive was a 'Metro' class 2—4—0 tank from Reading that was sub-shedded at Henley and returned to the parent depot each week for boiler washouts and inspections. The locos were changed on Sundays, a light engine (facing towards London) arriving at about 4.00 p.m. in the charge of a Reading crew who took the new loco on shed and then worked the remainder of the day's services on the branch with the previous week's loco before returning it to Reading. The reason for this arrangement was that one of the Henley branch crews worked from 8.00 a.m. to 5.00 p.m. on alternate Sundays in order that the other had a rest day.

During the week the shedman booked on at 11.00 p.m. each evening and the branch crew left the loco alongside the water tower for disposal and booked off. A reasonable fire was left in the firebox in order to maintain a good head of steam with which the shedman could drive the water pump in order to replenish the water tower. The fire was, however, relatively low because it was about to be thrown out and consequently the shedman often had quite a struggle to maintain enough steam to drive the pump for the period required and at the same time keep up the level of water in the boiler.

When the water tower was filled, the shedman eased the loco forward to position it alongside the end of the coal siding. The loco coal wagon was pushed along to the end of the siding right up to the loop, so that the coal could be shovelled directly into the bunker. The loco was then moved over to the shed siding for disposal. The fire was cleaned and much of it was thrown out before the loco was moved over to the front of the pit just inside the shed. Here the ash pan was raked out and the smoke box cleaned before the loco was finally stabled at the end of the track inside the building.

The fire that remained under the doors at the back of the firebox was covered over with fresh coal and, with the damper open, the smoky mass was left to pull through. The drop in temperature in the firebox obviously brought about considerable contraction, often resulting in a leaking tube plate which had to be kept under surveillance.

During the rest of the night, the shedman cleaned the loco, starting below the footplate with the frames and motion, followed by the brass and paintwork. After this he shovelled out the ashes that had previously been emptied into the front of the shed pit.

This was a dismal duty, working alone through the night, but if his work was carried out quickly enough during the early part of his shift, it was possible to sleep through his official mealbreak and often longer.

The early turn fireman booked on at about 5.45 a.m., spread the small fire over the bars and gradually built it up. When the driver arrived later the fireman closed the front damper so that he could oil the big ends and pack the spindle glands, then, with the drain cocks open, the front end of the shed was filled with steam as the fireman eased the locomotive forward into an appropriate position to facilitate the remainder of the oiling. When this was completed the tanks were filled alongside the water tower in readiness for the day's services. After the war, the crews

'Metro' class 2—4—0T No. 616 near the water tower at Henley c.1930.

Reg Daniells

secured overtime by booking on at 3.00 a.m. each weekday morning during the winter for carriage warming purposes. This was in order to pre-heat the stock for the two London through trains. At 4.00 a.m. the branch pannier collected one rake of coaches and drew up to the other so that the loco was sandwiched in between. It then remained there until 6.30 a.m. during which time the driver apparently played cards with the signalman in the box.

The first train down the branch in the morning was the Henley goods which left Reading West junction at 4.35

123

a.m., arriving at Twyford at 4.51 a.m. The wagons for Twyford were left in the yard there and at the same time the Henley goods brake van, No. 3257, was picked up for return to that station and apparently put on the front of the train.

The goods left Twyford for Henley at 5.48 a.m., calling at Wargrave and Shiplake on the way to set off the appropriate wagons. The empty wagons from Shiplake had to be collected on the 'down' journey and taken on into Henley as the yard was only served by a trailing connection from the 'down' line and therefore could only be serviced by trains travelling in that direction. The small yard was busy and usually packed, so shunting at Shiplake could take some twenty minutes or so. If, as often happened, the shunting was not completed in the scheduled time, the goods train had to be backed across the trailing crossover on to the 'up' line and held there to allow the passage of the 6.37 a.m. newspaper and parcels train which it then later followed to Henley.

The newspaper train from Twyford was worked by a light engine from Reading which arrived at Twyford at 6.20 a.m., collected the appropriate vehicles, and ran to Henley as the 6.37 a.m. This was closely followed by a second engine from Reading which ran light engine all the way to Henley, arriving there at 7.00 a.m. to work out the 8.18 a.m. later on.

The first train out of Henley was the 7.07 a.m. passenger train to Twyford which left from platform No. 1 and was worked by the Reading engine that had arrived with the newspaper train.

The locomotive worked two local return trips over the branch, the second being the 7.55 a.m. from Henley, before eventually working the 8.50 a.m. Henley to Paddington.

Rejoining the branch loco and crew, they collected the branch coaches from the loop siding, under the overall roof, hauled them up to the signal box and propelled the train back into the platform No. 1. This train worked out as the 7.27 a.m. which returned as the 7.57 a.m. from Twyford.

During later years, there had been occasions when the branch locomotive had insufficient steam pressure in time to work its first duty. When this had been the case, Driver Les Babbage had been known to borrow the Reading goods loco to perform the first duty, leaving the Reading crew to eat their breakfast in the goods brake van. As already mentioned, the 7.55 a.m. to Twyford was worked with the Reading engine and crew.

The branch crew returned with the 7.57 a.m. from Twyford arriving at Henley in platform No. 1. The branch engine came off the train and took water but the stock worked out again at 8.18 a.m. hauled by the second engine that had previously arrived from Reading. Quite why this locomotive had arrived so much earlier is a mystery although it probably allowed for carriage warming during the winter months and also provided a 'standby' loco at Henley.

Having completed the two return passenger trips over the branch, the first Reading engine then came off of the branch coaches and, taking water first, collected a rake of some eight or nine coaches from the sidings and finally departed with the 8.50 a.m. businessmen's through train

to London. Before this time and certainly in 1919, this train had conveyed the slip portion off the 5.15 p.m. from Paddington which had arrived at Henley the previous day.

The branch engine then made its second trip of the day with the 3 coaches that formed the 9.15 a.m. to Paddington which the Henley loco and crew worked as far as Maidenhead. Here the coaches were attached to the 9.18 a.m. from Marlow and taken on to London. The branch engine took water at Maidenhead before returning as a light engine to Twyford. Apparently a sign at the water column there declared that the water was only for use by locomotives on the Wycombe branch, but the small branch engine had a limited water capacity and so the crews understandably ignored the ruling. Meanwhile back at Henley, the second Reading engine had returned with the 9.20 a.m. from Twyford and, presumably after taking water, left with the 10.00 a.m. through train to London, which again consisted of a further rake of some eight coaches that were collected from the carriage sidings. Commencing on 2nd June, 1930, the 9.15 a.m. from Paddington to Taunton slipped a coach at Twyford, which was then taken on to Henley by the branch engine, which returned from Maidenhead at 9.55 a.m. and departed from Twyford at 10.02 a.m. Prior to this, the 10.02 a.m. is believed to have been run with coaches that were already stabled at Twyford. On arrival at Henley, it ran into platform No. 2, and, after putting the stock away in the sidings, the loco took water and worked out again with the 10.45 a.m. to Twyford, with the coach set that it had originally started with from platform No. 1.

A light engine from Reading had arrived at Twyford at 10.00 a.m. and continued from there to Henley, tender first with a single coach collected from the gas tank siding, as the 10.42 a.m. from Twyford. This was a 'Hall' class turn at this time which, after arriving at Henley, again into platform No. 2, left the coach in the carriage sidings and worked out with the 11.10 a.m. through train to Paddington. The stock for this train was later (commencing on 2nd June, 1930) the return of the slip portion off the 9.15 a.m. from Paddington to Henley the previous day.

The next two arrivals at Henley followed in quick succession. The first was part of a through train that left Paddington at 10.00 a.m. for Windsor and Henley and arrived in platform No. 1, and the second was the 11.00 a.m. auto train from Reading which arrived in platform No. 2. The auto train departed again at 11.32 a.m., but the locomotive from Paddington left what was usually a four coach suburban set in the carriage sidings, and remained on the branch to work the 12.12 p.m., 1.16 p.m. and 1.58 p.m. local trains to Twyford with the branch set previously conveyed as the 10.00 a.m. from Twyford.

Until about 1926, an Oxford locomotive was used on this turn, usually a 'Flower' class 4—4—0, after which time the motive power came from Reading.

The branch goods was busy shunting at Henley throughout the morning and was booked to leave at 11.45 a.m. The departing train was made up in the bay platform, against a Reading brake van or 'Toad', but, in cases of extreme congestion in the yard, it had been known to use platform No. 2 for this purpose. Excessive shunting sometimes delayed the departure of this train which then had to be rescheduled to fit into the timetable.

Churchward mogul No. 4379 crossing from the main to relief line at Twyford East with a fast train for Henley on Sunday, 19th June 1927.
M. W. Earley

On its way to Twyford the goods ran straight through Shiplake but called at Wargrave to pick up empties and arrived at Twyford at 12.10 p.m. On arrival the train drew into the 'up' relief platform and then reversed down the line into the 'up' refuge siding, setting the brake van off into the yard on the way. The yard was then shunted, during which time the private siding at Twyford Mill was also serviced, the latter apparently often receiving some five or six wagons.

Shunting the yard at Twyford could take any amount of time as the layout there necessitated running out on to the 'up' relief line during the execution of each movement. This effectively meant that sorting could only be carried out between trains on that line and unavoidably much of the time was simply spent waiting in the yard.

When the shunting operations were completed, the outgoing wagons and the brake van were propelled down to the refuge siding and coupled on to the rest of the train, the whole of which was then hauled into the 'up' relief platform again. The loco ran round to the other end of the train and then departed for Reading, crossing over to the 'down' relief opposite Twyford West signal box, the booked time of departure being 4.00 p.m.

Returning to Henley again, after the departure of the goods, the Reading engine, as already mentioned, worked out with the 12.12 p.m. and the branch engine, after a lay over of some 1¼ hours at Twyford, returned with the 12.15 p.m.

The branch coaches were gas lit and the gas cylinders were recharged in the bay at Twyford probably between 11.00 a.m. and mid-day services. The supply came from a gas tank wagon or 'Cordon' that was stabled in the gas

siding and was carried over to the bay by means of pipes that were laid across the track bed under the rails. A carriage and wagon examiner travelled from Reading each day to carry out this work.

The branch engine worked out again with the 12.55 p.m. and returned with the 1.19 p.m. from Twyford, after which the loco went over to the shed and pumped water, while the Reading engine maintained the branch services which were run in and out of platform No. 1.

Two auto trains leaving Reading at 12.55 p.m. and 1.50 p.m. also ran into Henley, using platform No. 2, and departed again at 1.33 p.m. and 2.20 p.m. respectively.

Having completed the three return trips over the branch, the Reading engine made its final departure with the 3.05 p.m. to Twyford. After arrival there, the coaches were stabled in the gas siding and the loco returned light engine to Reading at 3.45 p.m.

Meanwhile, the late turn branch crew had booked on at Henley at 2.30 p.m. and, with the pumping completed, had prepared the engine to recommence the day's duties. The branch coaches were collected again and, after the arrival of the 2.05 p.m. from Paddington, the fresh crew worked out of Henley with the 3.30 p.m. to Twyford which departed from platform No. 1.

The 2.05 p.m. from Paddington for Henley and Wycombe was hauled by a Slough engine, often a '36XX' class 2—4—2T, leaving Twyford at 3.05 p.m. and arriving in platform No. 2 at 3.17 p.m. The coaching stock was left in the 'up' sidings and a new train was formed with two branch coaches, fitted vans collected from the goods shed and the Henley branch 'Toad'. The Slough engine and crew then departed again with the mixed train at 3.50

p.m. At Twyford the coaches were stabled in the 'down' relief siding, the wagons and goods brake left in the goods yard and the loco worked on to Reading as a light engine, leaving Twyford at 4.36 p.m. The vans left in the yard were later picked up by the Old Oak Common goods, known as 'The Fly' which started at Reading West Junction at 4.20 p.m., arriving at Twyford at 5.04 p.m. and departing from there at 5.25 p.m.

The branch train returned from Twyford again at 3.56 p.m., running into platform No. 1 and departed again at 4.25 p.m.

The next arrival at Henley was a portion of the 3.35 p.m. from Paddington for Henley and Aylesbury. The Henley portion left Maidenhead at 4.20 p.m. and Twyford at 4.31 p.m., and is believed to have again been worked by an engine from Slough. This was followed by the arrival of the 4.43 p.m. auto train from Reading which arrived in platform No. 2 and left again at 5.27 p.m., after the return of the branch train with the 5.10 p.m. from Twyford. The 5.20 p.m. auto train from Reading left Twyford at 5.31 p.m., crossing the previous one at Wargrave, and remained on the branch to provide the 5.58 p.m. and 6.50 p.m. return services from Henley to Twyford and back before finally returning to Reading with the 8.05 p.m.

The branch engine left its coaches at Henley and worked out to Twyford again as a light engine, closely following the Reading auto train. At Twyford this engine collected four coaches that were detached from the 5.15 p.m. Weston-Super-Mare train from Paddington and returned to Henley with them, leaving Twyford at 5.56 p.m. In earlier years the Henley portion of the 5.15 p.m. had been slipped at Twyford.

The Maidenhead train, which was still at Henley, worked out as the 5.48 p.m. through train to Paddington and had in the meantime left Henley, followed ten minutes later by the Reading auto train to Twyford.

On its return to Henley, the branch loco put the stock of the 5.15 p.m. in the carriage sidings and collected the branch coaches to work the 6.18 p.m., 7.05 p.m., 8.45 p.m., 9.32 p.m. and 10.27 p.m. trains to Twyford.

The 6.15 p.m. through train from Paddington, for Windsor and Henley, arrived in No. 2 platform at Henley at 7.10 p.m. The coaches from this train were left in the 'up' carriage sidings for the following morning and the loco, which was supplied from Reading shed, worked out tender first with a mixed train of milk vans and one passenger coach for Reading, leaving the bay platform at 7.30 p.m.

The second through train from Paddington left there at 6.38 p.m. and arrived at Henley at 7.40 p.m. The coaches from this train were also left in the 'up' carriage sidings, and the loco returned light engine to Reading at 8.30 p.m. The locomotives from these London trains were turned at Henley before leaving for Reading but from the early 1930s or thereabouts the locos returned tender first up the branch and were turned at Reading shed in readiness for the following morning.

The 7.40 p.m. from Paddington for Worcester and Wolverhampton slipped three coaches at Taplow which combined with a portion of the 5.05 p.m. from Paddington, which had also previously been slipped at Taplow,

continued to Henley in the charge of a Slough engine, arriving at the terminus at 8.43 p.m. This train later worked out again to Paddington at 9.25 p.m.

The last auto train from Reading arrived at Henley at 9.42 p.m. but, instead of simply returning to Reading, this time provided a through service to Maidenhead which left Henley at 9.58 p.m.

The 10.27 p.m. from Henley was the last return trip of the day made by the branch train, which arrived back in platform No. 1 at 10.57 p.m. The locomotive ran round the coaches, which were then hauled out of the platform and stabled in the loop siding under the roof. The locomotive was then handed over to the shedman and the crew booked off. Before concluding, however, after a long interlude, one more train worked over the branch into Henley, this being a final through train from London which left Paddington at 12.15 a.m., Mondays excepted, and arrived at Henley at 1.28 a.m. This train worked out again as empty stock, leaving Henley at 1.40 a.m. and stopping at Wargrave for the guard to extinguish the lights there and lock up the station.

Excursions and Special Trains

Henley, as a popular Thameside resort, attracted a great many excursions and special trains over the years, quite apart from the regatta traffic, but excursions from the town were also arranged.

A regular excursion that actually started from Henley was the annual church choir outing, which certainly ran from as early as 1894 and is believed to have continued into the 1930s. These trains picked up passengers at Shiplake and Wargrave and were well patronised, conveying members of numerous church choirs from the local area to various destinations which included Bournemouth, Brighton, Eastbourne and Margate. The stock usually consisted of some ten coaches or so hauled by a Southern loco over that company's territory.

Sunday excursions that were also run from Henley throughout the 1930s to Weymouth, Torquay, Weston-Super-Mare and Barry Island, actually started from Ealing. Passengers from Henley joined the trains at Twyford and were taken there in the branch train, which returned to Henley as empty stock and ran in to Twyford again in the evening to collect them.

On one such occasion, a 15 coach excursion to Weymouth was so full when it reached Twyford, which was the last pick-up point, that it was decided to attach the two branch coaches (Nos. 7218 and 7219) complete with passengers, to the existing train to provide the necessary accommodation. However, these vehicles were non-corridor stock and the branch passengers had to travel all the way without any lavatories.

The loco hauling this train was a 'Castle' class 4—6—0 but, because of the additional load, the Reading 'down' station pilot, a 'County' class 4—4—0, was coupled on and double-headed the train from there to Weymouth.

On the return journey, the smaller 'County' class loco returned with nine of the coaches, which included the Henley vehicles, and the 'Castle' followed with the remaining eight.

As already mentioned, the combined rail and river excursions that were run to Henley during the summer

The guard waits while *Pendeford Hall* is watered at Henley one Sunday lunch time c.1930. Having worked in with a through train from Paddington, the loco was turned and stabled on one of the pit roads, where it was left in readiness for the return journey that evening.

Reg Daniells

months began in 1902. During the early 1920s, two trains were run regularly into Henley from Paddington on Sundays. When the passengers had left the train, the empty stock was propelled into the 'down' sidings, which were of course empty at this time of the year. The loco was then driven over to the loco yard and watered and turned before being stabled on the pit sidings radiating from the turntable. The locomotives from each train remained there ready to work their respective trains back later and the crews booked off duty for a couple of hours

The crew of the same train about to book off duty for their riverside stroll. They are, from left to right, Fireman Leaks, Guard Curtis and Driver Stenner.   *Reg Daniells*

and frequently strolled along the river until it was time to return.

In later years there was only one such train on Sundays and, instead of waiting, the crews returned 'on the cushions' and a fresh crew was sent later for the return working.

During the early 1900s, a through service from Victoria was run on Sundays during June and July. The train left the SE&CR and GWR joint station at 9.48 a.m. and ran to Henley via Clapham Junction, Battersea, St. Quintin Park and Wormwood Scrubs, calling at Taplow, Maidenhead, Wargrave and Shiplake to set down passengers, arriving at Henley at 11.08 a.m. This service was usually hauled by a 'Metro' class 2—4—0T. The return service left Henley at 8.10 p.m. in the evening.

Other Sunday excursions included trips from Cardiff and Newport to Goring from where passengers continued by steamer along the River Thames to Henley where they rejoined their train which had worked through to Henley as empty stock. These excursions were run occasionally during the 1930s and were usually hauled by 'Hall' class locomotives.

Before leaving this chapter, one interesting excursion that has been recorded was run by the Southern Railway from Bournemouth to Henley on 18th August, 1929. The train of Southern stock was hauled right through to Henley by an 'Lll' class 4—4—0 No. E164 with a Great Western pilotman from Reading on the footplate. The passengers travelled by steamer along the Thames to Windsor where they rejoined the train which worked there from Henley as empty stock.

Regatta crowds at Henley station in 1907.

H Nicholls courtesy Royal Photographic Society.

CHAPTER SEVEN

HENLEY REGATTA

'At all times a scene of interesting animation, Paddington station affords, during a few mornings in July of each year, a spectacle of remarkable vivacity and colour. These favoured mornings are those of the Henley Regatta, and from shortly after nine o'clock to close upon noon each day the great station is thronged by hundreds of young men and maidens attired in the lightest and brightest of boating costumes. The spirit of the gay boating carnival seems to be in the air and 'special' after 'special' runs out from under the great cylindrical roofs packed with 'river men' and fashionable ladies.

'Henley station, too, is naturally a scene of activity. Hundreds of holiday people meet the trains, everyone looks sunburnt and happy, and excitement is in the air. The Regatta is an epoch of thrilling enjoyment for Henley; a period of dense crowds, and a place full to overflowing.'   *GWR Magazine, 1908.*

HENLEY Regatta is held over a course which is unique in that it runs perfectly straight for over a mile. The event originated from the first university boat race which was held between Hambleden Lock and Henley Bridge in 1829, although the Regatta was not established until 1839 and, in fact, began as something of a local fete to attract visitors to the town.

In 1851 HRH Prince Albert became patron of the Regatta which thereafter became known as Henley Royal Regatta. Later in 1857 the opening of the railway made it far easier for large numbers of visitors to reach the town and so from what was a rather modest beginning, the Regatta grew in popularity and importance to become the world's premier rowing festival.

Thousands of visitors travelled to Henley for the event, to the mutual benefit of both the town and the railway company. The intensive service required to cope with the

Regatta crowds arriving at Henley in 1914.   *GWR Magazine*

extraordinary traffic obviously required a great deal of planning, in some ways more reminiscent of a military campaign. Some of the details of the arrangements made for the 1902 event, typical of that period, are given below. They reflect an age when the railway was Britain's principal means of passenger travel and special efforts were made to cater for events of this nature. They also give an interesting insight into railway operation of the period.

Each morning special through trains ferried the crowds from Paddington to Henley, with return workings for the

empty stock. Later in the morning many of the coaches were stabled in the extensive sidings in readiness for an equally intensive evening service back to London. The 1902 event was held on Tuesday, Wednesday and Thursday, 8th, 9th and 10th July. The special timetable scheduled 26 trains (27 on Thursday) from Paddington to Henley each day, 12 of which ran non stop to Henley. Of the 26 return trains (28 on Thursday) 12 ran non stop to London, some calling at Ealing Broadway. The timetable also included through trains from Windsor, Didcot and Oxford. 'Up' goods and coal trains were 'kept back' between Didcot and Reading 'so as not to leave Reading between the hours of 9.0 a.m. and 1.0 p.m., and 4.0 and 10.30 p.m.', and no ballast or chalk trains at all were permitted between Reading and London on the days concerned.

Staff were drafted in from all over the system to cope with the extra workload. They came from as far afield as Hereford, Wrexham, Bradford-on-Avon, Chester, and Liskeard and were employed both on the branch and main line. Extra signalmen were also provided in the London cabins and twelve additional ticket collectors were required at Paddington. The table below shows the additional staff required for station and signalling duties on the branch. The guards shown in this table were used on station duties and further men were required for train working duties.

	Henley	Shiplake	Wargrave	Twyford
Inspectors	6	1		1
Ticket Collectors		8		4
Clerks	4	2		1
Tel. Clerks	2			3
Porters	26	2	1	5
Policemen	6			3
Foremen	4			
Signalmen	4	1	1	3
Lampmen	3			
Passenger Guards	1			1
Van Guards	1			
Goods Guards	1			
P.W. Men	2 gangs			
Groundmen/ Handsignalmen	6	3	2	10
County Police	5			

Geo. Bushell & Son

An Edwardian regatta scene.

The intensive service required modification of the standard signalling regulations on both the Main/Relief and Branch lines at Twyford. Handsignalmen were provided at all home and distant signals of both Twyford 'boxes to enable safe relaxation of normal block signalling requirements. An additional up stop signal was also provided on the branch '387 yards from the Twyford West Box Up Branch Home Signal'. It was worked from that box on regatta days and a flagman was stationed at it to protect trains which were stopped there. The signalbox at Mill Lane, which is thought to have been out of regular use by this time, was also opened during the special timetable to provide an additional block section.

Handsignalmen were provided at distant signals on the branch to repeat the signals in accordance with the Instructions for Fog Signalling and were obviously an additional safeguard during the intensive service. However, this practice does give rise to speculation that the A.T.C. trials on the Henley Branch (chapter 4) were conducted with more than their commonly accepted aims in mind. Even prior to 1914 the provision of seven extra men at the distant signals would have been a considerable expense, which the provision of A.T.C. could avoid.

Goods traffic for the branch was curtailed as coal and mineral traffic was not worked to Twyford or Henley after Saturday, 5th July, all unimportant goods being held back at Didcot until after the regatta. At Henley, where space was at a premium, the sidings were cleared and all wagons worked out of the terminus on the Monday evening. General goods only were still transported on a goods train which arrived at Henley (ex Reading) at 6.25 a.m. and was entirely unloaded by two gangs of P.W. men in order to release the trucks immediately.

Before the erection of the ticket barrier at Henley, when tickets were collected at Shiplake, a temporary timber office was erected there each year on the 'up' end of the platform. This was used as a mess for the team of ticket collectors. At one time a sleeping car was provided at Henley to accommodate the ticket inspectors. This vehicle was stabled in the loop siding under the verandah where apparently another coach provided office accommodation for the extra clerical staff. A further coach was also stabled at the end of the coal siding alongside the engine shed for the team of porters.

Another temporary building was erected each year on the edge of the station forecourt at Henley. It was used as

Henley station concourse in a quieter moment between trains during the 1907 regatta.

Horace Nicholls, courtesy Royal Photographic Society

More visitors arriving for the regatta, this time in 1902.   *G. W. Reeves, courtesy Miss S. Reeves*

a parcels office into which the parcels and relevant staff were evacuated from the main building. For some years a section of the iron railings enclosing the western boundary were removed and the building erected on the adjoining site (now occupied by a car park). Later, during the 1920s, a portion of the adjacent auction rooms was used instead with a ramp leading from the station forecourt to a side door. The reason for the evacuation of the parcels office was to provide a large cloakroom and left luggage office to serve the thousands of visitors, although the decline in visitors using the railway in later years made the provision of the temporary building unnecessary and the second room from the south end of the main building, which was used as a bicycle shed until 1948, was pressed into service as an additional cloakroom. For many years the goods yard was utilized as a car park for regatta visitors. It was particularly well patronised on Saturdays but one of the regular relief staff remembers only five cars being parked there in the 1920s, when the station forecourt was used for the purpose.

During the event the little market town was transformed into a mecca for oarsmen from all over the world. It was enthusiastically decorated with flags and bunting draped over many of the buildings and suspended across the main streets, and all the local hostelries were filled to capacity.

A glance at any of the accompanying photographs conjures up visions of hot summer days with hundreds of fashionable men and women swarming out of the station with the arrival of each special train. This was surely the age of elegance with England still at the peak of her Imperial wealth and power, when the populace could look forward to a brighter future in blissful ignorance of the 1914-18 carnage.

The endless succession of high spirited and impeccably attired visitors were attended by 25 extra porters and both railway and county police were on duty to watch over the proceedings and, according to the working notice, 'move on any loafers'. Henley had become a vital part of the social calendar, whether one was actually interested in the events or simply wished to enjoy strolling along the ancient banks of the glorious Thames amidst the contagious excitement.

One always associates those far off summers with glorious weather and in 1902 the first day of the races was indeed fine. However, it rained the following afternoon and there was a thunderstorm on the Thursday evening. The number of passengers carried on each day was 7,270, 11,120 and 16,711 respectively, making a total of 35,101. This was a net decrease of 1,472 on the previous year's figures, apparently due to a smaller number of people travelling on the first day, and despite the weather, there was actually a marginal increase on the second and third days. The figures quoted were apparently based on 'countings in the trains at which the tickets were collected, namely Paddington, Twyford and Shiplake'. They are, however, considerably higher than those quoted in the table relating to the company's subscription to the regatta!

The number of passengers increased in subsequent years until the 1906 regatta, after which the number of visitors attending by rail declined. In 1910 the Management Committee of the Henley Regatta wrote to the GWR asking them, in view of the mutual interest involved, to increase their subscription to the event for 1911 as they represented that the state of the finances of the event was so serious that the very continuance of the event was at stake.

The company first subscribed to the event in 1888 when a sum of £10 was given. Then from 1889-1900 inclusive an amount of £20 was subscribed annually. The following table shows the subscriptions related to the traffic from 1902-1910 inclusive.

Year	No. Passengers	Total amount £	Subscription £
1901	25,927	6,992	50
1902	25,668	7,154	50
1903	29,240	6,495	50
1904	30,327	6,519	50
1905	29,867	6,532	75
1906	31,280	6,497	75
1907	22,859	4,635	75
1908	23,021	4,681	75
1909	20,078	4,176	50
1910	15,137	3,000	50

The reversion to £50 had been made in 1909 because of the falling off in traffic but following the Regatta Committee's request the company resumed its £75 subscription.

The Management Committee again approached the GWR the following year for a further increase in their subscription to the sum of £100 in view of the exceptional nature of the event that year which was to be attended by their Majesties King George V and Queen Mary.

The regatta was held that year between 3rd and 6th July and was attended by the King and Queen on the day of the final events. The King and Queen arrived by a special train that left Paddington at 11.20 a.m. on Saturday, 6th. On arrival at Henley they walked from the station to the State barge in which they journeyed to the course.

The company continued to subscribe to the event and in 1930 gave a donation of £25.10s.0d. The improved weather conditions that year resulted in increased carryings, the receipts amounting to £1,041 compared with £974 in 1929. The number of tickets collected at Shiplake for Henley was 18,600, an increase of 2,795 over 1929. However, this must have been an exceptional year as from 1931-34 the GWR's contribution was only £10.00 and from 1935-39 £12.00. After the war the regatta donation was revived with a donation of £20.00 in 1946.

According to the 1902 instructions, the branch train for the occasion comprised a brake third, a first, a second, two compos, two thirds and one van. A spare train of eight six-wheelers was also kept on standby at Twyford and pilot engines were provided at both Twyford and Henley. In later years the additional locos necessary for the extensive shuttle service between Reading and Henley were borrowed from Worcester and Bristol and allocated to Reading shed. These were mainly 'Metro' class 2–4–0Ts.

A faded but rare glimpse of the station frontage in 1912, showing the canopy erected for the visit of King George V and Queen Mary.
Courtesy Miss S. Reeves

Two views of the decorations for the 1952 regatta.

British Railways

Fresh locomotives were coupled onto the opposite end of the trains when reversing direction at Twyford, thus saving time and avoiding the need to run round each train on the main line.

An additional locomotive was stabled at Henley in the entrance to the shed for the sole purpose of maintaining the water supply in the main tank opposite, in order to serve the needs of the many visiting locos in addition to the normal requirements. The locomotive, which is known to have been a 'Barnum' class 2—4—0 on a number of occasions, was coupled to the small pumping engine alongside the water tower by means of specially laid pipework that ran under the tracks between the pumping house and the engine shed. The loco remained there all day, acting as a stationary boiler fitted with a 'Not to be moved' sign.

A signalman was put on turntable duty and in many cases the locos that arrived on the special trains from Paddington, after being watered and turned, remained at Henley until required for the return journeys in the evening. The loco yard was small for this kind of stockpiling and locos were stabled on the two pit sidings radiating from the turntable, the loco coal road alongside the engine shed and even in the loop that ran in front of the signal box.

As demand lessened, special regatta services accordingly decreased. In 1953, for instance, there were only three special trains from Paddington to Henley during the mornings of Wednesday 1st and Saturday 4th July, and only two on the Thursday and Friday. Even so the line was still busy with relief trains running between Reading and Henley and empty stock workings, all of course in addition to the regular timetable. The branch train was strengthened to four coaches and the usual railcar service from Reading was replaced by a two coach auto set.

The arrangements included the seven coach Radley College specials which, starting from Oxford, ran straight through from Radley to Henley on Wednesday and Saturday. A turnover engine was also still provided at Twyford at this time, but only on the last day when a pilot engine was also posted at Henley. Finally, to ferry the crowds back to London after the last race there was a choice of six through trains leaving Henley at 5.35, 6.40, 7.20, 8.30, 10.35 and 11.55 p.m.

In subsequent years the service gradually declined until by the late 1960s only one through train was provided. The removal of the passing loop at Shiplake in 1968 led to timetabling difficulties even for this level of service. The solution adopted that year was to run the return service non-stop from Henley to Twyford — the first time that such a daytime working had occurred over the branch for many years. By the mid 1970s the through train from Paddington was running only on the Saturday and Sunday.

The station frontage during the 1955 event. *British Railways*

'Metro' class 2—4—0 No. 976 at Henley during the early years of the century. The driver standing alongside is Albert Gardiner. He transferred to Henley in 1902 and remained there until he retired in 1934 after 44 years service with the Great Western. The fireman has not been identified.

Courtesy P. Pengilley

CHAPTER EIGHT

LOCOMOTIVES & STOCK

I T seems that '517' class 0—4—2Ts were allocated to Henley for branch passenger services during the closing years of the 19th century, although little evidence of loco working has been found for the period between the demise of the broad gauge and 1900. 1902 was the last year that members of the class were regularly shedded at Henley, the official allocation for 1901-2 including Nos. 531, 568, 829, 1471 and 1482. They were replaced by 'Metro' class 2—4—0Ts but nevertheless later reappeared during the day's timetable on the Reading to Henley auto services.

Besides '633' class 0—6—0 No. 639, which was occasionally shedded at Henley during 1901-3, the 'Metro' class 2—4—0Ts came to be used almost exclusively on branch services right through to the early 1930s.

The official allocations for 1901-47 are listed in an appendix on page 175, but they should not be regarded as definitive. The official records tend to show the locomotives nominally based at a sub-shed over any given period but if, as in the case of Henley, the locomotives were exchanged with the parent shed on a weekly basis for washouts etc., the alternating locos are not recorded.

Locomotives were frequently moved around the system and some changes shown in the records are remarkably diverse. In 1909, for instance, 'Metro' class 2—4—0 No. 982 was at Henley in February, transferred to Truro the following month, then on to Falmouth before returning to Reading in May. It reappeared at Henley in July and remained there for much of the rest of the year.

The predictable allocation took an unusual turn at the end of 1928 when '36XX' class 2—4—2Ts, Nos. 3605, 3610 and 3614, took over the branch services. They were, however, short-lived at Henley and indeed may have been intended only to stand in while the regular 'Metro' class tanks, Nos. 615 and 616, were reconditioned at Swindon. They were both returned to the branch during the spring of 1929 but their condition was evidently assessed while they were away and they were later withdrawn in February 1931. A more unlikely locomotive, 'County' class tank No. 2237, was also used on the line for a while in 1930 prior to its withdrawal the following May.

The familiar 'Metro' tanks were replaced with a '3901' class 2—6—2T No. 3915. These locomotives were converted from the '2301' class tender engines, although they

'517' class 0—4—2T No. 1482 at Henley in 1902.

G. W. Reeves, courtesy Miss S. Reeves

'Metro' class 2—4—0T No. 616 pumping water at Henley c.1930.

Collection J. E. Kite

received new frames, boiler, tanks, etc., this particular engine being rebuilt from No. 2493 in 1908. This loco-motive was not at all popular with the branch crews and it was much to their relief that it was withdrawn in May 1932.

'57XX' class 0—6—0PTs were allocated to Henley during the 1930s but, although they were destined to become a very familiar sight, they still alternated with other types at this time. In 1934 0—6—0PT No. 2747,

which often worked from Reading with the branch goods, was shedded at Henley and, for a short period from the end of 1935 until the beginning of the following year, 'Metro' class 2—4—0T No. 3585 also worked the branch. It had just been sent to Reading freshly repainted from Swindon and is reported to have been the first 2—4—0 shedded at Henley since 1930 and possibly the last regular example to be so. Although this loco remained at Reading, the branch services continued to be worked by '57XX'

'Metro' class 2—4—0T No. 615 at Henley, again c.1930. This loco, alter-nating with No. 616, was regularly shedded at Henley. The driver is Fred Clarke while the fireman (in the cab) is Les Babbage. Les joined the company at Plymouth in 1916 and, because of the shortage of staff during the Great War, was quickly made up to fireman and transferred to Henley the following year. Apart from a few years at Llanelly where he transferred to take up his first driving position, and some three years at High Wycombe, he remained at the branch for the rest of his career, spending the last few years before his retirement in the 1960s, driving the branch railcar.

Reg Daniells

'36XX' class 2—4—2T No. 3614 connected to the water pumping engine at Henley in 1929.

Reg Daniells

class 0—6—0PTs, No. 9722 being shedded at Henley during the early part of 1936, with No. 9758 standing in during washouts. '48XX' class 0—4—2Ts were tried on the branch from the spring of 1936, but although they were auto fitted, the regular branch coaches were retained and the locos ran round the train at each end of their journey. The 0—4—2Ts thereafter alternated with the '57XX' class panniers until the end of the war when the '57XX' finally dominated the scene. They lasted until the withdrawal of steam-hauled passenger services in 1958 although a number

'3901' class 2—6—2T No. 3915 at Henley in 1932. *Reg Daniells*

0—6—0PT No. 8721 at Henley in the early 1930s. *Reg Daniells*

of the more modern '94XX' class 0—6—0PTs were used on the line throughout the 1950s, at least partly at the wish of the senior driver who found them to his liking and particularly requested their retention whenever possible as they were found easier to maintain.

Amongst the '57XX' 0—6—0PTs allocated to Henley between 1940 and 1958 were Nos. 3662, 3663, 3679, 3715, 4606, 4649, 4661, 4688, 5751, 5763, 5766, 5722, 5772, 7708, 7777, 7788 and 9773 whilst '94XX' class 0—6—0PTs included Nos. 8430 and 9403, both of which were regular, and Nos. 9404, 9411, 9412 and 9413.

One of the modern 94XX class panniers No. 9403 awaiting departure with a branch train at Henley in the early 1950s.

Lens of Sutton

Establishing the development of the branch locomotives allocated to Henley has been a relatively simple task in comparison with that of tracing the numerous classes that have appeared on the branch over the years on other duties. Henley was a 'red' route, a colour code which referred to the weight restriction imposed by the strength of the bridges over a particular route. In the case of Henley, this effectively meant that only the 'King' class 4—6—0s were too heavy for the line. Consequently, the busy timetable provided for a wide range of locomotives that were used over the years, in addition to which empty stock working to the carriage sidings at Henley brought about the unusual appearances of such locos as 'Aberdare' and '28XX' classes.

Locomotives appearing on services other than the local branch train have generally been traced back to the early 1920s and in order to simplify the information the following notes have been divided into the duties performed.

London Through Services

A small number of the locomotives used on through trains between Henley and Paddington in earlier years provide at least some insight to the service at that time. These include:

1894 Standard Goods No. 1199.
1896 Standard Goods No. 791, 'Metro' class 2—4—0T Nos. 1405 and 1419, and Dean Goods No. 2332.
1897 'Metro' class 2—4—0 No. 626.
1898 'Metro' class 2—4—0 No. 623 and Standard Goods No. 679.

An unidentified 2—4—0 departing from Henley with a through train to Paddington in 1902.   *G. W. Reeves, courtesy Miss S. Reeves*

1906   'Metro' class 2—4—0T No. 1404 and '36XX' class 2—4—2T Nos. 3601, 3610, 3611 and 3615.

1910   'Barnum' class 2—4—0 No. 3225.

'Duke' class 4—4—0s from Reading shed regularly worked out the 8.50 a.m. 'up' through train from Henley to Paddington during the early 1920s and included Nos. 3254 *Cornubia*, 3256 *Guinevere*, 3281 *Cotswold*, 3283 *Comet*, 3284 *Isle of Jersey*, 3286 *Meteor*, 3288 *Mendip*.

The 'Dukes' were gradually replaced on these services by 'Bulldog' and 'County' class 4—4—0s which included 'Bulldog' class Nos. 3309 *Maristow*, 3321 *Brasenose*, 3346 *Godolphin*, 3367 *Evan Llewellyn*, 3386 *Paddington*, 3390 *Wolverhampton*, 3391 *Dominion of Canada*, 3394 *Albany*, 3405 *Empire of India*, 3410 *Columbia*, 3413 *James Mason*, 3434 *Joseph Shaw*, 3446 *Goldfinch*, 3448 *Kingfisher*, 3452 *Penguin*, 3453 *Seagull*, 'County' class Nos. 3813 *County of Carmarthen*, 3814 *County of Chester*, 3827 *County of Gloucester*, 3829 *County of Merioneth*.

During the 1930s the new 'Hall' class 4—6—0 locomotives gradually displaced the older 4—4—0s at Reading, hauling the 'up' through trains to London and, more occasionally, Churchward 'Moguls' appeared at Henley on these trains, the latter including Nos. 4384, 5323, 6354, 6356, 6378 and 7300.

Before the Second World War, 'down' through services were hauled by locomotives shedded at Old Oak Common. 'City' class 4—4—0 No. 3718 *City of Winchester* was very much a regular on this service during the 1920s as was 'Atbara' class 4—4—0 No. 4138 *White* which was fitted with a Westinghouse pump. Other locos included 'Atbara' class No. 4130 *Omdurman*, 'Bulldog' class 4—4—0 No.

3429, again fitted with a Westinghouse pump, 'County' class 4—4—0s Nos. 3820 *County of Worcester*, 3821 *County of Bedford*, 3838 *County of Glamorgan* and '63XX' class No. 6332 which was also fitted with a Westinghouse pump.

'Bulldog' class 4—4—0 No. 3319 *Weymouth* at Henley in the late 1920s. The names were removed from a number of the class to avoid confusion with train destinations. This particular loco lost its name in May 1930 and was withdrawn two years later.

Reg Daniells

'Star' class 4—6—0 No. 4023 *King George* in the loco yard at Henley during the regatta service on 2nd July 1914.
W. L. Kenning, courtesy Adrian Vaughan

'Star' class 4—6—0 No. 4013 *Knight of St. Patrick* alongside the engine shed at Henley, probably on the same day but certainly during the regatta. The loco is stabled between two others, that in front being Churchward mogul No. 4328 which was apparently booked to work a 6.15 p.m. special to Paddington.

W. L. Kenning, courtesy Adrian Vaughan

'63XX' class mogul No. 6333, from Cardiff Canton, taking water at Henley on 3rd July 1954.   *Pat Moffatt*

'2221' class 4–4–2T 'County' tanks Nos. 2244 and 2250 were also used, but their limited water capacity could prove to be a problem for the crews over the distance.

While Ranelagh Bridge turntable, just outside Paddington station, was being rebuilt during the late 1920s, a variety of locos were used on the Henley services, apparently for about a three week period, during which time 4–6–0 'Saints', 'Courts' and 'Stars' appeared on the branch.

The 10.00 a.m. from Paddington, which left coaches at Slough for Windsor, was at one time worked with an Oxford engine and included such regulars as: 'Flower' class 4–4–0s Nos. 4153 *Camellia*, 4160 *Carnation*, 4166 *Polyanthus*, 'Badminton' class Nos. 4101 *Barrington*, 4102 *Blenheim*, 4110 *Charles Mortimer*, 'Atbara' class Nos. 4129 *Kekerwich* and 4141 *Aden*. After about 1926 the locomotives for this turn were provided from Reading shed, and included 'Bulldog' class Nos. 3319 *Weymouth* and 3411 *Stanley Baldwin*.

No. 7906 *Fron Hall* at Henley on 6th July 1962. Having worked into Henley with the second evening train from London, it was coupled to the loco from the earlier service already waiting in the loop alongside Cold Bath footpath, before departing 'light engine' for Reading shed.

Pat Moffatt

No. 6981 *Marbury Hall* heading away from Wargrave one morning with one of the through trains to London.   *J. F. Russell-Smith*

The 'Moguls' and new 'Hall' classes displaced many of the older 4—4—0s and were working the 'down' services to Henley by about 1930. On 1st May, 1931, No. 3712 *City of Bristol*, the last survivor of the 'City' class at that time, worked the 6.38 p.m. from Paddington to Henley with 12 eight-wheeled coaches. This must have been one of her last duties as she was withdrawn later that month. 'Moguls' appearing at Henley on the services included Nos. 6340, 6354, 6356, 6389, 7300 and 7319.

Eventually, after 1930, the through services in both directions were worked by locomotives from Reading shed and 'Castle' and 'Hall' classes became the regular motive power rostered for these turns. A great many of these larger 4—6—0s, including the occasional 'Star', appeared at Henley over the years. In fact, in January 1943 the *Railway Observer* reported that 62 different 'Castles' had appeared at Henley during the preceding 18 months period. 'Castle' class Nos. 4085 *Berkeley Castle* and 5034 *Corfe Castle* saw regular service on the 10.20 a.m. to London in 1950-51, but of the large number of locomotives that appeared on through services between Henley and Paddington, some of the more regular included 'Hall' class Nos. 4939, *Littleton Hall*, 5973 *Rolleston Hall*, 6960 *Raveningham Hall*, 6968 *Woodcock Hall*, 7919 *Runter Hall*, 'Castle' class Nos. 5036 *Lyonshall Castle* and 5038 *Morlais Castle*. On a number of occasions in 1958 or thereabouts, 'Britannia' class Pacifics hauled the 7.48 a.m. to Paddington, including No. 70020 *Mercury* and during the final years at least one of the 'County' class 4—6—0s appeared on one of the evening through services.

A local girl, Miss Peggy Challis, poses on the footplate of '517' class 0—4—2T No. 570 at Henley on 16th May 1934. The loco is on one of the auto services from Reading and the driver is Alfred Lovell.
Reg Daniells

Reading—Henley Auto

The earliest known regular locos employed on these services, at least so far discovered, are '517' class 0—4—2Ts that ran auto trains into Henley during 1924 and 1926. These were No. 833 which ran in a brown livery to match the coaches, and No. 531, which apparently came from Aberdare. It had a round-topped firebox and was painted in the maroon livery.

'Metro' class 2—4—0Ts Nos. 1455, 1459 and 3564 were used in 1925 and during the late 1920s No. 1430. On 25th November, 1929, No. 3599 was sent to Reading, fitted with auto gear, and used on the Henley auto service to replace No. 1430 which was sent to Swindon works.

No. 526, had been away at Swindon and was returned to Reading at the end of 1931 fitted with a Belpaire firebox. This loco, together with Nos. 570 and 574, then worked the auto services until they were later replaced with the new Collett 0—4—2Ts, the first of which to arrive new at Reading was No. 4827 in November, 1933, just after No. 526 was withdrawn in September. Nos. 570 and 574 were both withdrawn the following year.

It is probable that most of the Collett 0—4—2Ts allocated to Reading shed appeared at Henley on this service, particularly in the event of diesel railcar failures which are said to have been frequent. The 1938 allocation included Nos. 4807, 4809, 4817, 4820, 4837, 4842, 4844, 4847, and 4862. Since 1948 Nos. 1407, 1444 and 1447 (renumbered) worked the 10.20 p.m. from Reading.

Steam railmotors were also regularly used on this service during the 1920s and '30s and these included Nos. 41, 62, 64, 72, 84, 85, 87, 93, and 98. No. 37 was probably one of the last that was still in use at Henley in 1934-5 and was withdrawn in June 1935. Diesel railcar No. 1 called at Henley between 1.16 and 1.34 p.m. on an extensive working that was introduced in 1934. However, by the summer

Driver Alfred Lovell again *(right)* on an earlier occasion, with another '517' class on the same service.

Reg Daniells

of 1937, No. 1 was no longer in the district but various diesel railcars thereafter were used on the Henley Auto and included Nos. 12, 15, 16, 18, 19 and in later years No. 1, which again worked on the line from about 1948 and on into the early 1950s.

Henley Goods

'1016' class 0—6—0PT No. 1026 was shedded at Reading and regularly worked the Henley branch goods during the early 1920s, followed by '27XX' class 0—6—0PT No. 2757, which was employed on this duty from about 1924 until 1927. Other locomotives occasionally rostered for this duty at that time included '1076' class 0—6—0PTs Nos. 1241 and 1293, '2021' class 0—6—0PT No. 2086, '27XX' class 0—6—0PT No. 2747 and apparently 'Barnum' class 2—4—0s. The 'Barnums' are said to have

Converted 'Metro' class 2—4—2T No. 3593 standing in the 'down' relief refuge siding at Twyford with an auto train on the Henley, Reading and Maidenhead route on 20th July, 1927. The locomotive was the only one of its class to be converted to this wheel arrangement and was withdrawn later that year. The coaches were the very distinctive Clifton Down stock converted for auto working.

M. W. Earley

Railcar No. 1 at Henley during its second spell on the Reading to Henley service during early BR days, photographed on 13th May 1950.

S. Fletcher

Collett 0—6—0 No. 2248 in the bay at Henley with the branch goods on 18th March 1964.

Reg Daniells

made regular appearance on this duty but were not at all popular with the crews because the screw reverser, with which the locos were fitted, was laborious during the extensive shunting operations throughout this long duty. In contrast, the famous 'Dean goods' 0—6—0s were ideally suited to the work, always highly regarded amongst the crews and came to be used during the late 1920s, in particular Nos. 2305 and 2340.

In 1937 it was recorded that two '57XX' class 0—6—0PTs alternated between the branch goods and branch passenger services but it is not known how long the practice continued.

In 1940 No. 1758 was reported to have regularly worked the turn which at that time, possibly as a wartime arrangement, included one passenger trip to Twyford and back first thing in the morning.

During the post war years '57XX' class pannier tanks continued to be used on the goods service with the occasional '94XX' class making an appearance. Churchward 'Moguls' were also used on this duty but, during the 1960s, Collett '2251' class 0—6—0s became the most regular, supplemented by the occasional 'Manor' and even 'Hall' class 4—6—0s.

Branch Passenger Stock

During the 1920s there were two sets of passenger stock for the branch, one of which appears to have been in use on the line for many years. This set comprised two 38′ 6″ bogie brake thirds, Nos. 2061 and 2062, which were coupled to each end of a pair of four-wheeled composites, Nos. 7864 and 7865. The brake thirds were built in 1895, on secondhand underframes and wheels, to diagram D15 as part of Lot 766. The four-wheelers were also completed in 1895 and built to diagram U4 as part of Lot 763. (2061 and 2062 were withdrawn in 1938 and 1932 respectively.)

The other coaches allocated to the branch were three eight-wheeled low roof brake composites, of which Nos. 7217 and 7218 usually ran as a pair, leaving No. 7219 spare. These vehicles were being used as brake thirds at this time but were originally built as 2nd/3rd class brake

An unidentified '57XX' 0—6—0PT in the yard at Henley c.1931.

W. Y. George

composites to diagram E51 as part of Lot 813. These were completed in 1896 as Nos. 1217-19 but were later renumbered in 1907.

Certainly since the Second World War, two pairs of converted slip coaches were used on branch services. These were mainly 'toplight' vehicles but at least one 'concertina' type was used, as illustrated opposite. The slip gear had been removed from these vehicles but the end windows were retained. For some time after Nationalisation these coaches kept their GWR chocolate and cream livery and, until they were repainted in the new BR livery of crimson and cream, ran with the simple addition of a 'W' prefix to the number of each vehicle. The pairs of coaches alternated in use each week and whichever became the spare set was stabled at the end of the bay platform for cleaning.

During the last years of steam-hauled services the slip coaches were replaced by 70 ft composite No. W7940W and 57 ft brake third No. W5798W. The compo was built in 1924 to diagram E111 as part of Lot 1319 while the brake third, which dated from 1934, was built to diagram D118 as part of Lot 1510.

The local branch train leaving Henley on 26th March 1948. The coaches are converted 'toplight' and 'concertina' slip coaches.

S. Fletcher

Two more converted slip coaches stabled in the bay at Henley on 13th June 1953.

Pat Moffatt

No. 5076 *Gladiator* passing near Wargrave Piggot School with one of the morning through trains from Henley to Paddington.

J. F. Russell-Smith

CHAPTER NINE

THE END OF AN ERA

The last years of steam 1948-63

THE Nationalisation of the railways had little effect on the branch at first, but the steady growth of road transport had far reaching effects which, particularly following the post-war depression, brought about many changes and inevitable cutbacks under the new régime.

New British Railways liveries were being applied to locomotives and rolling stock and gradually infiltrated on to the branch, but the first structural evidence of BR ownership at Henley was the provision of station name-boards at the end of each platform. Prior to this, rather unusually, the name of the station had only been displayed on small glass nameplates affixed to the head of each lamp. The nameboards were enamelled in the Western Region colours of chocolate and cream and mounted between reinforced concrete posts, presenting a very functional appearance. The glass nameplates were also replaced at this time by small enamelled plates secured to the posts of the lamps along the platforms.

The signal box at Wargrave had long ceased to be of any real use and, not surprisingly, was closed and the

signals removed on 3rd October, 1954. The 'down' trailing crossover to the yard was also removed and the remaining connection controlled by a single lever ground frame released by an Annett's key instrument from Shiplake.

The trackwork at Henley was simplified over a two week period in July, 1956, and the station was extensively resignalled at the same time with the old timber post signals being replaced by tubular steel post varieties illustrated in the photograph on page 153. The station platforms were subsequently renumbered at some time before 1959 but the date has not been established. The No. 3 bay platform, which was on the 'down' side of the line, became No. 1 and in doing so finally fell into line with standard GWR practice of geographically following the platform numbering sequence at Paddington. This must have caused some confusion at Henley after all those years. Enamelled signs were provided inside the station to replace the old wooden ones and to indicate the new platform numbers, and in July 1956 the station was completely repainted in Western Region colours in time for the line's centenary the following year.

No. 4019 *Knight Templar* at Henley awaiting departure with the 10.20 a.m. to Paddington on 5th August 1948. The locomotive was withdrawn the following year.
W. A. Camwell

'57XX' class 0—6—0PT No. 9749 at Henley on 1st August 1955.

J. N. Faulkner

No. 6991 *Acton Burnell Hall* at Henley with a Radley College Regatta Special on 1st July 1954. The locomotive ran tender first to Twyford in order to face the direction of travel for the rest of the journey along the main line.

Pat Moffatt

The station noticeboard bore a chalk-written declaration of the line's survival of 100 years for the benefit of the passengers, and a short article appeared in the local press. The line had originally been opened in time for the Henley Regatta and appropriately the decorations for the 1957 event incorporated a large panel on the front of the entrance hall at Henley heralding the celebration. At the same time, however, the declining traffic over the years brought about a complete reversal of the prosperity that had led to the doubling in 1897, and, during the latter part of 1957, plans were prepared for the singling of the branch in order to effect necessary economies. However, the work was not put in hand at this time.

Steam hauled branch services were withdrawn in 1958 and replaced by new diesel railcars; the steam-hauled auto services and the ex GWR railcars were also withdrawn.

The last steam hauled branch train ran on Sunday, 5th October, when 0–6–0PT No. 9404 hauled the usual two coach train, comprising coaches Nos. W5798W and W7940W, and as usual a light engine, No. 9749, was sent from Reading to work the evening services from 5.00 p.m. until 11.00 p.m., detonators being fired nearly every time trains left Henley. The new diesel railcar, No. W55000, was supplemented by No. W55013 or No. W55018 from Reading. The 7.48 a.m. and 8.48 a.m. through trains to London and their return services from Paddington at 5.15 p.m. and 6.15 p.m., together with the branch goods, continued to be steam hauled at this time.

A memorable occasion in the town's recent history occurred on Wednesday, 8th April, 1959, when the Queen visited Henley. She had travelled from Windsor to Banbury that morning by Royal train and later to Henley by road.

The simple chalk-written notice heralding the line's centenary.

A. E. Bennett

The Royal train worked from Banbury to Henley as empty stock, arriving at 1.15 p.m. The branch was suitably spruced up for the occasion and Henley station was decorated with flowers. The Queen boarded the Royal train from platform No. 3. It left at 5.15 p.m., the 5.14 p.m. railcar to Twyford being rescheduled to depart at 5.33 p.m. The Royal train consisted of four coaches with brake compo No. 7372 leading, followed by saloon No. 9006, first No. 8003 and brake compo No. 7377, and was

A proud moment for Station Master Alec Livingstone as he escorts Her Majesty the Queen and the Earl of Macclesfield to the Royal Train.

British Railways

No. 5056 *Earl of Powis* heading the Royal Train out of Henley.

British Railways

hauled by 'Castle' class locomotive No. 5056 *Earl of Powis*. Another 'Castle', No. 5061 *Earl of Birkenhead*, was stationed at Henley as standby.

The Henley branch was singled as planned in two stages between 11th and 20th June, 1961. The work involved the removal of the 'down' running line and the first stage, which made this line redundant between Henley and Shiplake, was completed on Wednesday, 14th. A new signal box was opened at Shiplake on 11th June, and the first colour light signals were installed on the branch when the Henley 'down' distant, home and 'up' starting signals were replaced. The second stage between Shiplake and Twyford

was carried out between 17th and 20th June but at Twyford the 'down' running line was left in position between the junction and a point just north of the old Bath Road bridge where a new crossover was installed and beyond which the 'down' line terminated in a 100 ft long ash pile. The 'down' line served only to provide a facing connection from the 'down' relief line to the branch and had the advantage of providing what was, in effect, a crossing loop at Twyford, whilst the former 'up' line in fact became single line throughout.

Wargrave station was served by the former 'up' line only, the waiting room and 'down' platform being removed

No. 4977 *Watcombe Hall* joining the main line at Twyford with the 8.43 a.m. Henley to Paddington through train on 19th April 1960.

R. F. Roberts

in July, followed by the footbridge in September. At Shiplake the 'down' running line was retained and used as a passing loop. This was connected to the 'up' line by means of a new facing point installed immediately to the north of Lashbrook viaduct and another at the opposite end of the station south of the neck of the yard. Incidentally, the steelwork that had supported the 'down' line over the Thames and Lashbrook viaducts was left intact at this stage and not removed until 1965.

At Henley, apart from the colour light signals previously mentioned, alterations were minimal and involved only the provision of one additional facing point lock and the disconnection of the former 'down' line trailing connection from the 'down' sidings. No. 1 'up' carriage siding had been shortened prior to the singling work (possibly instead of relaying as this was the last siding that remained intact from 1897) and the new 'up' starting signal was sited on the former trackbed.

The new single line sections were provided with continuous track circuiting to enable their operation by acceptance lever working, thus avoiding the use of tokens and speeding operation. As mentioned later, the singling scheme also led to the removal of all ATC equipment on the branch.

As part of the Paddington to Reading scheme, a new signal box was opened at Twyford on 21st October, 1961. The new box had both a mechanical frame, to control the branch and other local connections, and a Western Region standard Integra mosaic 'entrance-exit' control panel which controlled the main and relief lines between White Waltham and the western end of Sonning Cutting. The ultimate intention was to transfer the area controlled by the panel to Reading panel signal box and to retain the lever frame for local control, but traffic circumstances changed dramatically in subsequent years and led to a considerable revision of the original plan. Incidentally, the Henley bay engine release crossover, which had survived the introduction of diesel multiple units working, was not transferred to the control of the new box and was subsequently removed.

The Henley branch was again selected as a testing ground for experiments with a new signalling installation that is believed to have been the first of its kind in the world.

In connection with the trial of the equipment, Henley station was completely converted to colour light signalling in December 1961. As with Twyford, a Western Region standard 'entrance-exit' control panel was provided to control the signalling and, although for short term economy the points and FPLs were still mechanically operated from part of the existing frame, the levers were fitted with electric locks and circuit controllers that were interlinked with the new electronic system and worked in conjuction with it.

The experimental installation was designed to test the use of solid-state transistorised electronics in a railway signal interlocking environment. Developed by Mullard Equipment Ltd under a contract awarded by the British Transport Commission, the new circuitry considerably reduced the use of relays and, apart from being more

Top: Henley signal box with modified windows on 21st April 1961. *Centre:* The short-lived tubular steel starting signals with one of the posts for the new colour light signals already in position on 29th April. *Above:* The new control panel on 30th August 1961 before being brought into use.

Pat Moffatt & British Railways

The 5.20 p.m. from Paddington approaching Mill Lane on 11th June 1963.   *Pat Moffatt*

compact, it was anticipated that maintenance costs would be reduced.

The equipment was designed to perform the normal point and signal interlocking requirements that are necessary to ensure the safe passage of trains. The electronic circuits were also designed to fail safe which meant that in the event of the breakdown of any electronic component the appropriate signals would automatically return to 'danger'.

The panel was operated in the normal way whereby in order to set a route, the signalman turned a switch at the entrance or commencement of the desired route and pressed an exit button at the termination of the same. If the route was proved free the relevant manual point levers were released, thus permitting the points to be set. Once the correct route was set through the points and all other interlocking requirements were proved, the signals cleared automatically.

Although the installation was scheduled to have been in operation by 11th December, 1961, the testing of the electronic equipment was considerably delayed by some initial problems and the equipment was not in full operation until at least two weeks later. Following further teething troubles the system settled down to reliable operation but, probably because of rapid advances in electronics, it was never repeated elsewhere although it contributed much experience to later developments in this field.

With these changes, the character and perhaps rather staid image of the line was rapidly changing but, regrettably, with the further demolition and modernisation which followed, the line was never to be the same again.

At Henley station the soft gas lighting was finally replaced with electric, and two rows of tall modern

One of the gas lamps, still in use in May 1963. They were replaced with electric lights on July 4th.

Pat Moffatt

concrete-posted lamps illuminated the platforms whilst the gas lamps were sold off to collectors.

There was no gradual infiltration of diesel locomotives on the Henley branch, in fact the London through trains were steam hauled continuously until Friday, 14th June, 1963. That evening the two through workings from Paddington, the 5.20 p.m. and 6.15 p.m., arrived at Henley in the charge of No. 5038 *Morlais Castle* and No. 6924 *Grantley Hall* respectively, each train consisting of eleven coaches. No. 5038 had worked out with the 8.38 a.m. and No. 6924 had worked the 7.46 a.m. that morning. After the stock was stabled in the carriage sidings for the following Monday morning, the two locomotives were coupled together and departed tender first for Reading for the very last time at 7.45 p.m., so ending 106 years of steam hauled passenger services on the branch.

The years which followed merely brought about further decline and in any case are beyond the intended scope of this history. During the first few weeks of diesel hauled London through services, apart from the branch goods, there was only the very occasional appearance of steam locomotives at Henley on empty stock workings at weekends. 'Western' and 'Hymek' class diesel locomotives first worked the London trains, eventually followed by Brush 'Type 4s'. Goods services were withdrawn from Monday, 7th September, 1964, the last train having left Henley at 9.45 a.m. the previous Friday. This was the last regular steam working to Henley.

The Beeching report on the reshaping of British Railways that was published in 1963 had foreseen the likely withdrawal of freight services, but the Henley branch did not feature in the list of proposed closures. However, the effects of Beeching policies and a new attitude to the running of the railways reflected on the Henley branch after 1963.

Apart from the siding removals resulting from the withdrawal of freight services, the scene at Henley was radically changed by the demolition of the engine shed, water tower, booking hall, goods shed and stables and the erection of a housing development on the site of the former loco yard and shops along the station frontage.

Subsequent years led to a further policy of rationalisation which brought about the withdrawal of regular loco hauled workings from the branch and in turn further layout reductions at Henley in 1969. The previous year a revised timetable had led to the abolition of the single line passing loop at Shiplake. By the mid 1970s the surviving through services to London were withdrawn but occasional subsequent timetables have seen a limited reintroduction of through trains in each direction on the weekday service.

As part of continuing modernisation the control of signalling on the branch was transferred to Reading in March 1972 and the signal boxes at Twyford and Henley were closed. Shiplake signal box survived until March 1973 as a ground frame to control the level crossing, after which the last semaphore signals on the line were recovered and the crossing itself was converted to the 'open' type.

In 1975 the station buildings and overall roof were demolished, leaving only the 1904 platform canopy still standing. However, despite these reductions the line itself has managed to survive into its 125th year.

No. 5038 *Morlais Castle* and No. 6924 *Grantley Hall* waiting to leave Henley on 14th June 1963, the last day of regular steam-hauled passenger services.

Pat Moffatt

APPENDICES

TABLE SHOWING COSTS OF BUILDING THE LINE

| | HALF YEAR ENDING | | | | | | | |
| | 31st Dec. 1854 | 30th June 1855 | 31st Dec. 1855 | 30th June 1856 | 31st Dec. 1856 | 30th June 1857 | 31st Dec. 1857 | 30th June 1858 |
	£ s. d.	£ s. d.	£ s. d.	£ s. d.	£ s. d.	£ s. d.	£	£
Works			46. 13. 4.	2,105. 0. 0.	3,395. 5. 0.	4,088. 0. 0.	7,452	419
Land & compensation			5,246. 10. 6.	2,809. 17. 10.	4,398. 14. 7.	31. 0. 0.	—	—
Permanent Way			—	—	1,725. 12. 4.	12,076. 0. 0.	1,453	119
Parliamentary & Law (inc. all claims)			618. 16. 1.	142. 16. 2.	—	—	—	—
Conveyancing (inc. vendors costs)			—	—	17. 16. 6.	53. 0. 0.	41	328
Stations and Sidings			—	—	38. 12. 0.	6,485. 0. 0.	3,127	1,352
Engineering			901. 4. 3.	315. 13. 9.	165. 15. 0.	612. 0. 0.	195	—
General			43. 4. 5.	51. 18. 3.	—	—	—	—
Interest			613. 14. 8.	646. 16. 3.	814. 18. 8.	1,103. 0. 0.	—	—
LESS amount received for land sold						225. 0. 0.		
CUMULATIVE TOTAL	£5,409. 8. 7.	£16,570. 3. 6.	£24,040. 6. 9.	£30,112. 9. 0.	£40,669. 0. 0.	£64,894. 0. 0.	£77,163	£79,383

TRAFFIC DEALT WITH AT STATIONS BEFORE THE SECOND WORLD WAR

STATION.	YEAR.	STAFF. Supervisory and Wages (all Grades).	STAFF. Paybill Expenses.	TOTAL RECEIPTS.	PASSENGER. Tickets issued.	PASSENGER. Season Tickets.	PASSENGER. Passenger Receipts including S.T. etc.	PASSENGER. Parcels & Misc. Number.	PASSENGER. Parcels & Misc. Receipts.	PASSENGER. Total.	GOODS Forwarded. Coal and Coke "Charged".	GOODS Forwarded. Other Minerals.	GOODS Forwarded. General Merchandise.	GOODS Received. Coal and Coke "Charged".	GOODS Received. Other Minerals.	GOODS Received. General Merchandise.	Coal and Coke "Not Charged" (Forwarded and Received).	Total Goods Tonnage.	Total Receipts (exclud'ng "Not Charged" Coal and Coke).	Livestock (Forwarded and Received).	Total Carted Tonnage (Included in Total Goods Tonnage).
Henley Branch. Wargrave	1903	4	248	3,810	32,736	*	2,228	10,424	496	2,734		3	151	249	977	1,113	1,786	4,279	1,076	—	371
	1913	4	235	4,671	34,452	363	2,786	17,727	678	3,464	11	—	280	334	1,513	808	2,201	5,147	1,207	—	396
	1923	5	879	7,669	39,469	593	5,591	7,962	444	6,035	7	39	111	790	764	697	2,366	4,774	1,634	—	347
	1929	5	759	5,751	26,096	862	3,718	5,733	242	3,960	7	17	82	541	1,859	376	2,001	4,883	1,791	—	229
	1930	5	752	4,387	25,194	1,007	3,383	5,146	216	3,699	—	—	37	582	199	329	1,829	2,886	778	—	221
	1931	5	713	4,297	24,574	995	3,176	4,380	182	3,358	—	—	60	615	453	375	1,743	3,246	939	—	202
	1932	4	711	3,898	22,208	957	2,915	4,333	167	3,082	—	—	91	684	309	302	1,612	2,998	816	—	186
	1933	4	632	3,895	26,472	887	2,874	4,792	199	3,073	—	—	72	677	124	333	1,523	2,729	822	—	217
	1934	4	639	4,100	27,779	752	2,799	4,642	155	2,984	—	—	79	691	297	301	1,636	3,004	1,116	—	198
	1935	4	631	3,735	28,098	555	2,860	4,547	80	2,940	—	—	52	739	151	285	1,645	2,855	795	—	205
	1936	4	655	4,007	27,230	552	2,697	4,891	90	2,787	—	6	29	1,090	944	292	1,502	3,773	1,220	—	208
	1937	4	659	3,856	25,338	632	2,756	4,994	104	2,860	—	—	31	876	462	264	1,415	3,048	996	—	227
	1938	4	646	3,910	24,828	733	2,828	4,629	91	2,919	11	—	30	850	486	247	1,175	2,799	991	—	219
Shiplake	1903	4	245	3,063	23,029	*	1,410	6,143	283	1,693	7	—	545	783	1,451	1,111	1,785	5,682	1,370	—	520
	1913	4	326	3,718	33,579	*	2,587	11,440	331	2,918	—	6	149	715	619	575	2,028	4,092	800	—	355
	1923	6	934	6,991	39,386	584	5,264	7,276	550	5,794	46	32	120	502	510	567	2,469	4,246	1,197	—	274
	1929	6	1,014	5,513	33,551	1,063	4,242	6,990	297	4,539	15	70	58	448	356	405	2,202	3,554	974	1	144
	1930	6	1,031	5,200	31,444	1,070	4,082	6,767	298	4,380	5	10	135	462	140	355	2,180	3,287	820	—	150
	1931	6	896	4,758	31,182	1,076	3,890	5,712	263	4,153	—	—	28	364	68	277	2,186	2,923	605	1	137
	1932	6	916	4,725	31,099	882	3,571	5,341	272	4,043	—	—	42	312	419	176	1,806	2,755	682	1	107
	1933	6	843	4,259	31,620	811	3,500	5,331	189	3,689	—	—	40	320	50	287	1,678	2,375	599	1	111
	1934	5	747	3,816	31,533	737	3,243	4,712	247	3,490	—	6	9	312	71	80	1,879	2,357	545	1	32
	1935	5	748	3,935	31,462	612	3,128	5,178	262	3,390	—	—	6	242	715	60	1,248	2,271	545	—	15
	1936	5	745	3,553	31,407	697	2,868	5,356	281	3,149	—	—	5	272	411	26	894	1,608	404	2	8
	1937	5	760	3,314	31,633	802	2,846	4,858	264	3,110	—	—	6	164	42	95	710	1,017	204	—	65
	1938	5	784	3,317	29,232	855	2,998	4,434	218	3,216	8	—	6	111	25	9	783	942	101	2	8
Henley-on-Thames.	1903	26	1,853	30,461	94,789	*	10,971	69,988	4,618	15,589	740	1,026	4,296	5,653	2,999	13,161	14,404	42,279	14,872	264	7,782
	1913	29	2,203	30,483	100,784	*	11,994	89,368	4,056	16,030	353	427	5,190	3,932	3,896	12,970	17,028	43,796	14,453	238	7,098
	1923	25	4,104	41,924	105,076	1,421	21,336	48,074	3,419	24,755	711	635	2,596	3,519	4,133	9,046	16,515	37,155	17,169	123	4,171
	1929	24	3,643	35,057	102,396	3,954	18,395	54,243	2,995	21,390	131	628	1,486	4,034	3,906	5,991	19,495	35,671	16,432	99	3,482
	1930	23	3,991	34,406	97,872	3,888	17,608	53,432	2,809	20,417	117	677	1,380	4,014	4,825	5,454	17,129	33,596	13,989	74	3,616
	1931	23	3,796	32,652	89,933	3,557	15,874	52,135	2,555	18,429	206	357	1,535	2,083	7,347	5,278	19,781	36,587	14,223	101	3,693
	1932	26	4,090	29,832	86,060	2,851	13,911	54,601	2,674	16,585	473	63	3,735	2,395	4,399	4,059	18,335	33,420	13,247	60	5,315
	1933	26	4,298	29,395	91,238	2,393	13,600	59,186	2,792	16,392	216	103	2,431	2,295	5,921	4,721	17,875	33,502	13,003	37	3,958
	1934	25	4,620	30,182	92,941	2,322	14,183	59,427	3,118	17,301	55	170	2,062	2,852	3,961	5,208	17,731	32,069	12,981	51	4,091
	1935	26	4,439	28,528	95,440	2,569	14,852	59,143	1,859	16,711	27	162	1,316	3,098	2,512	5,092	18,082	30,289	11,817	39	4,203
	1936	26	4,516	30,289	102,725	2,548	15,530	59,660	1,972	17,502	51	264	1,372	3,966	3,694	4,939	15,113	29,399	12,787	46	4,344
	1937	26	4,682	29,918	99,363	2,428	15,849	59,255	1,819	17,668	7	307	1,349	3,628	2,246	5,073	15,740	28,350	12,250	33	5,073
	1938	27	4,798	32,161	88,954	2,439	16,086	57,425		17,815	—	124	1,306	3,197	5,882	5,861	15,605	32,035	14,346	25	6,125
Total	1903	34	2,346	37,334	150,054	*	14,619	86,555	5,397	20,016	747	1,029	4,992	6,685	5,427	15,385	17,975	52,240	17,318	264	8,673
	1913	37	2,764	38,872	168,815	*	17,367	118,535	5,045	22,412	364	433	5,619	4,981	6,028	14,353	21,257	53,035	16,460	238	7,849
	1923	36	5,917	56,584	183,931	2,598	32,191	63,312	4,393	36,584	764	706	2,827	4,811	5,407	10,310	21,350	46,175	20,000	123	4,792
	1929	35	5,416	46,321	162,043	5,879	26,355	66,966	3,534	29,889	153	715	1,626	5,023	6,121	6,772	23,698	44,108	16,432	100	3,855
	1930	34	5,774	43,993	154,510	5,965	25,083	65,345	3,323	28,496	122	687	1,552	5,058	5,074	6,138	21,138	39,769	15,587	74	3,987
	1931	34	5,405	41,707	145,689	5,628	22,940	62,227	3,000	25,940	206	357	1,623	3,062	7,868	5,930	23,710	42,756	15,767	102	3,942
	1932	36	5,717	38,455	139,367	4,690	20,597	64,275	3,113	23,710	473	63	3,868	3,391	5,088	4,537	21,753	39,173	14,745	61	3,608
	1933	36	5,773	37,549	149,330	4,091	19,974	67,309	3,171	23,145	216	103	2,543	3,292	6,095	5,341	21,076	38,606	14,404	38	4,286
	1934	34	6,006	38,098	152,253	3,811	20,225	68,781	3,550	23,775	55	176	2,150	3,855	4,299	5,649	21,246	35,415	14,323	52	4,321
	1935	35	5,818	36,198	156,102	3,739	20,840	68,868	2,201	23,041	27	162	1,354	4,079	3,378	5,440	20,975	35,415	13,157	39	4,423
	1936	35	5,916	37,849	161,362	3,797	21,095	69,910	2,343	23,438	51	270	1,406	5,238	5,049	5,257	17,509	34,780	14,411	48	4,560
	1937	35	6,101	37,088	156,334	3,862	21,451	69,100	2,187	23,638	7	307	1,386	4,668	2,750	5,432	17,865	32,415	13,450	33	5,365
	1938	36	6,228	39,388	143,014	4,028	21,912	66,488	2,038	23,950	19	124	1,432	4,158	6,363	6,117	17,563	35,776	15,438	27	6,349

* Not available.

TWYFORD 'DEPARTURE' BUILDING 1845

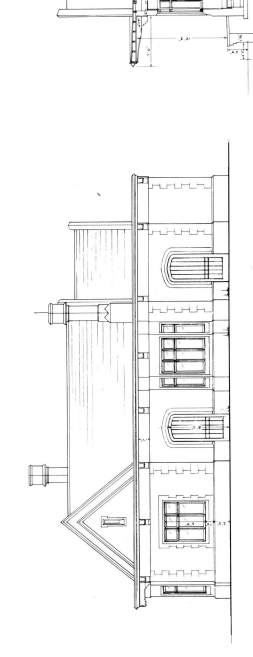

PLATFORM ELEVATION

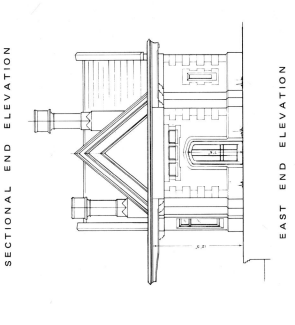

SECTIONAL END ELEVATION

EAST END ELEVATION

SCALE – 2 mm to 1 foot

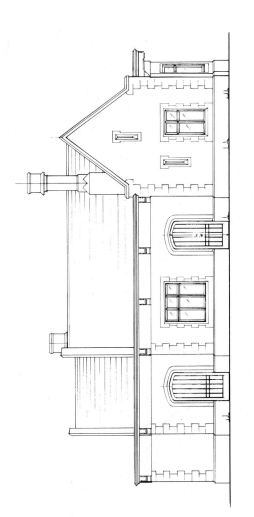

FORECOURT ELEVATION

Traced from original plans

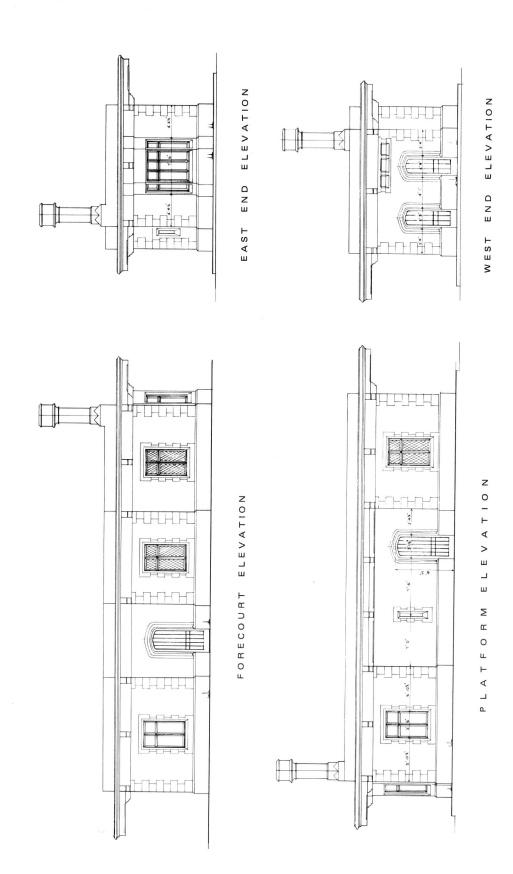

TWYFORD 'ARRIVAL' BUILDING 1845

EAST END ELEVATION

WEST END ELEVATION

FORECOURT ELEVATION

PLATFORM ELEVATION

SCALE – 2 mm to 1 foot

Traced from original plans

HENLEY BRANCH WAITING ROOM 1857

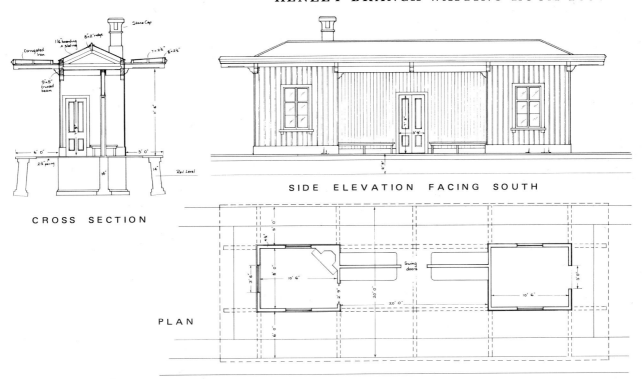

CROSS SECTION

SIDE ELEVATION FACING SOUTH

PLAN

SCALE — 2 mm to 1 foot

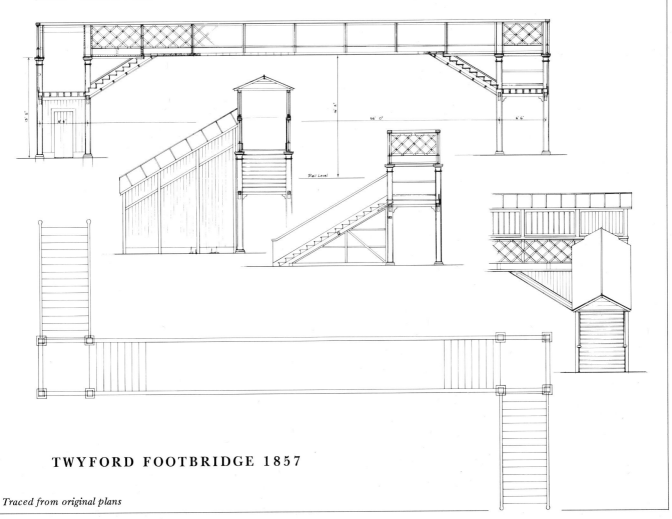

TWYFORD FOOTBRIDGE 1857

Traced from original plans

TWYFORD REPLACEMENT GOODS SHED 1857

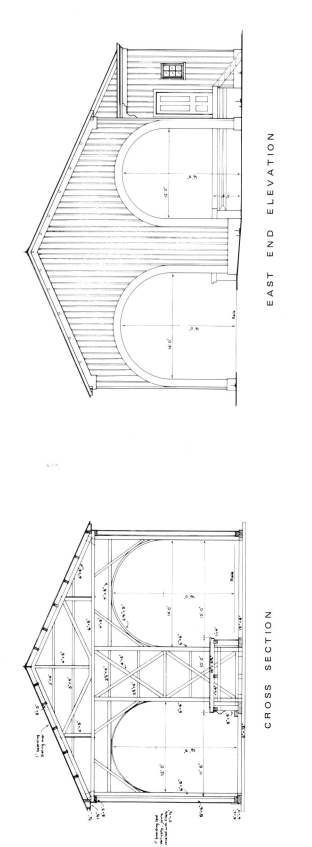

CROSS SECTION

EAST END ELEVATION

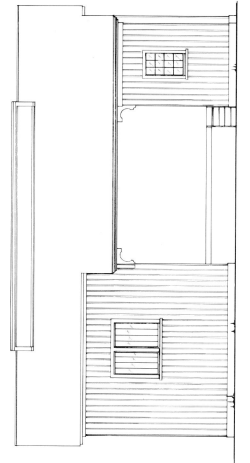

FORECOURT ELEVATION

SCALE – 2 mm to 1 foot

This drawing is also traced from original plans, but the elevations do not necessarily agree, particularly the semi-circular apertures.

161

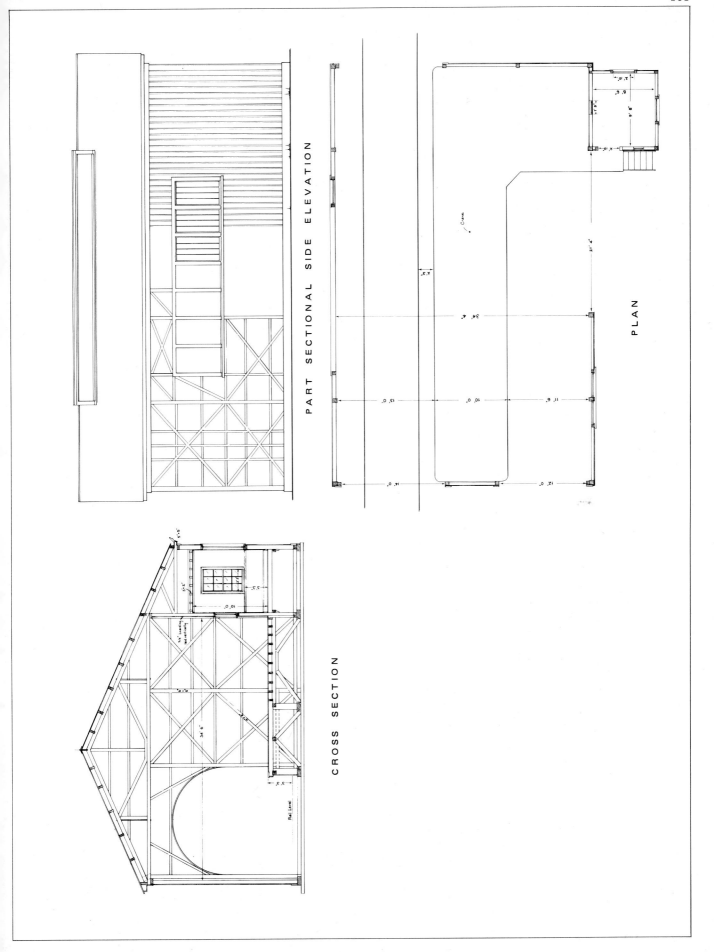

PART SECTIONAL SIDE ELEVATION

PLAN

CROSS SECTION

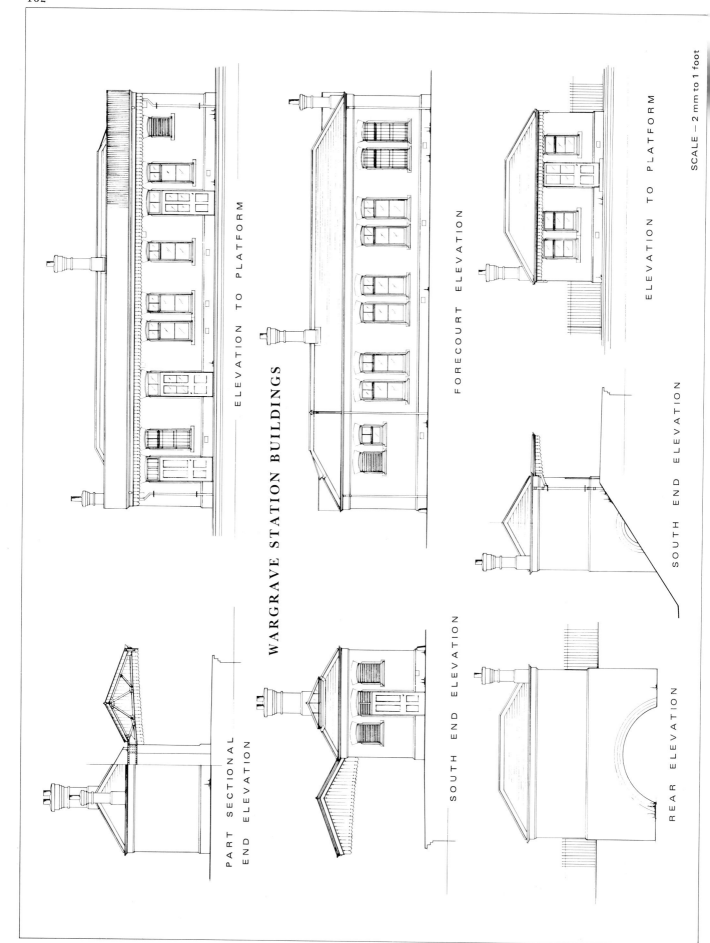

ELEVATION TO PLATFORM

WARGRAVE STATION BUILDINGS

FORECOURT ELEVATION

ELEVATION TO PLATFORM

SCALE – 2 mm to 1 foot

PART SECTIONAL
END ELEVATION

SOUTH END ELEVATION

SOUTH END ELEVATION

REAR ELEVATION

WARGRAVE SIGNAL BOX

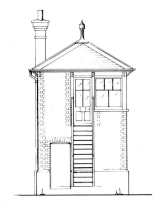

SOUTH END ELEVATION

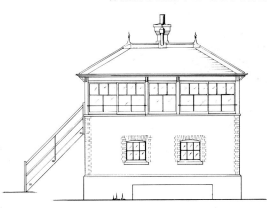

FRONT ELEVATION

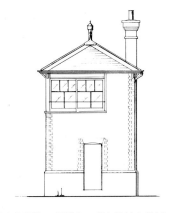

NORTH END ELEVATION

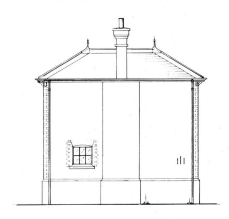

REAR ELEVATION

SCALE — 2 mm to 1 foot

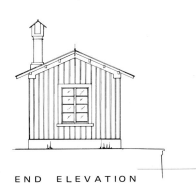

END ELEVATION

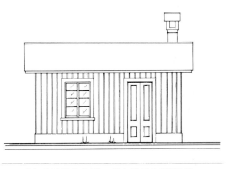

PLATFORM ELEVATION

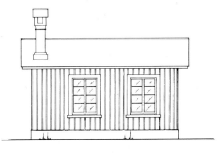

REAR ELEVATION

This building was designated for use at Wargrave in 1857. However, as there are no other references to any such station originally, and no trace of any plans for Shiplake, this was probably the Shiplake building.

SCALE — 2 mm to 1 foot

Traced from original plans

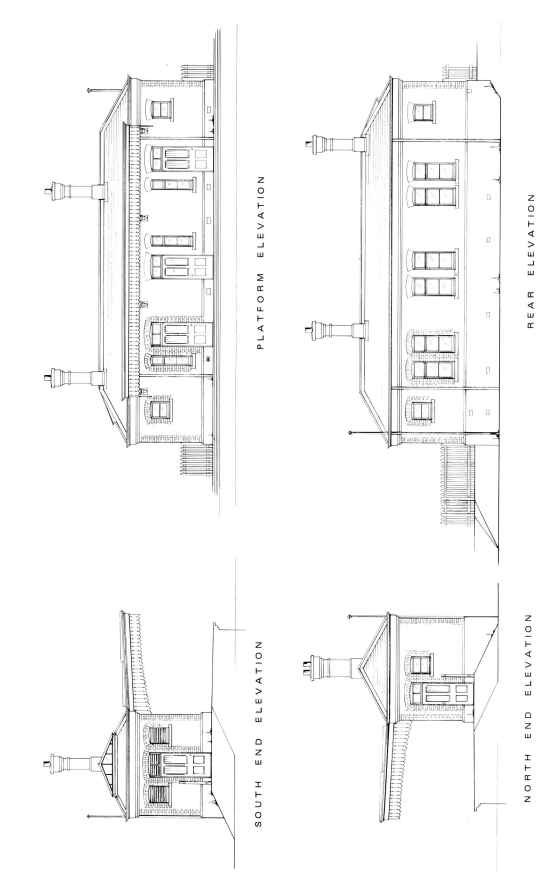

SHIPLAKE REPLACEMENT STATION BUILDING 1891

SCALE – 2 mm to 1 foot

PLATFORM ELEVATION

REAR ELEVATION

SOUTH END ELEVATION

NORTH END ELEVATION

SHIPLAKE LOCK-UP 1891

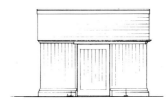

SHIPLAKE LAMP SHED 1891

SHIPLAKE FOOTBRIDGE 1897

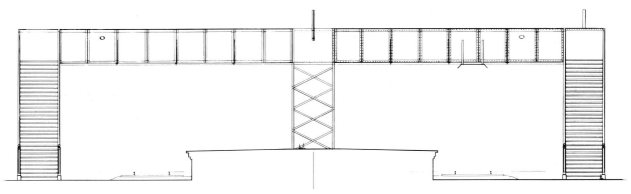

ELEVATION TO NORTH

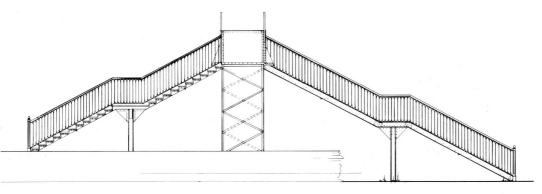
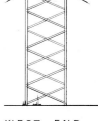

PART SECTIONAL CROSS SECTION

WEST END
ELEVATION

SCALE — 2 mm to 1 foot

HENLEY STATION

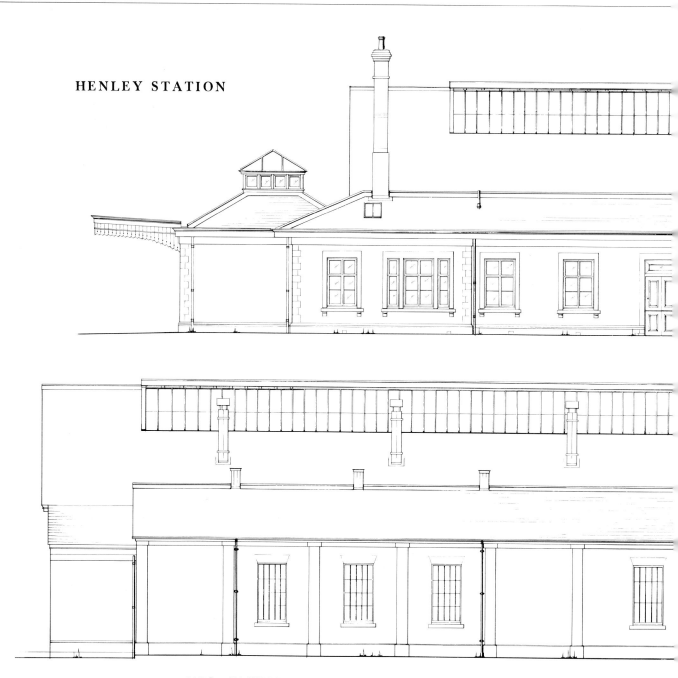

SIDE ELEVATION SHOWING ENGINE SHED

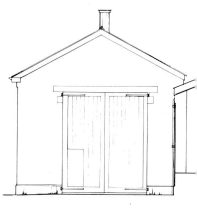

The drawings of Henley station are based on site surveys and show the station in its final form.

FORECOURT ELEVATION

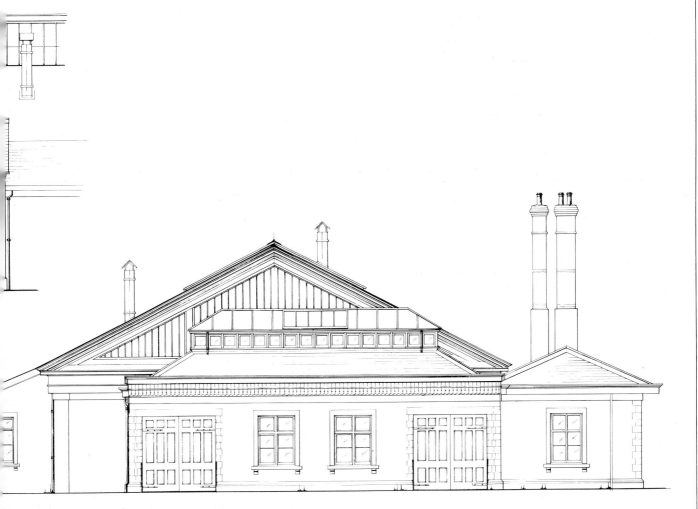

END ELEVATION FACING NORTH

SCALE — 2 mm to 1 foot

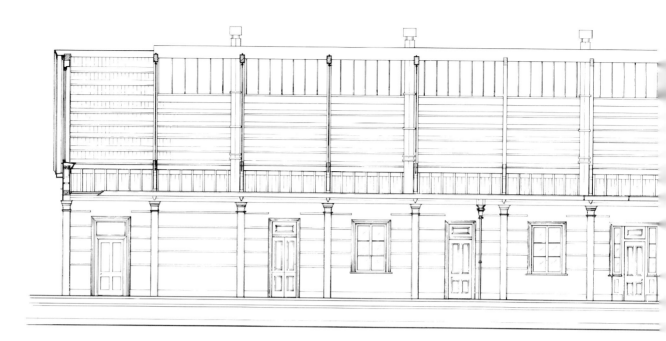

SIDE ELEVATION IN SECTION

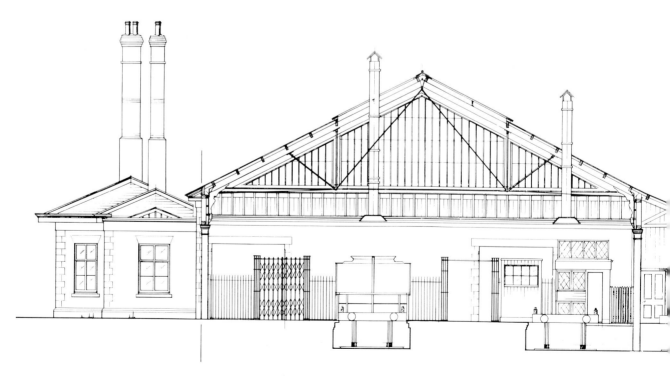

PART CROSS SECTION

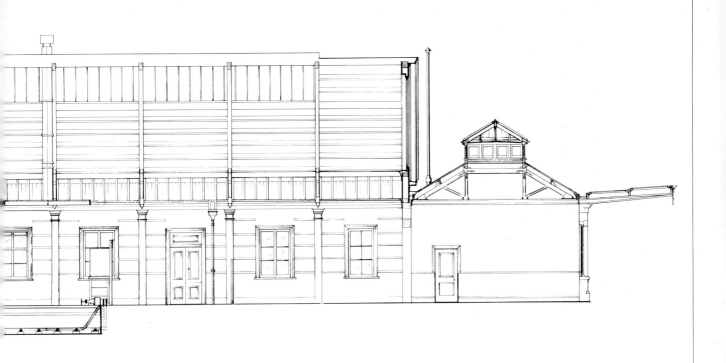

1904 PLATFORM CANOPY

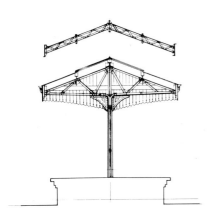

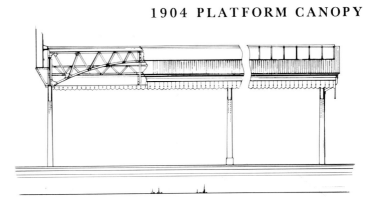

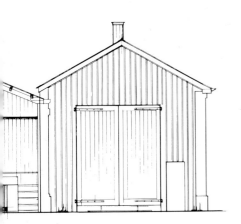

SCALE — 2 mm to 1 foot

WAREHOUSE AT HENLEY

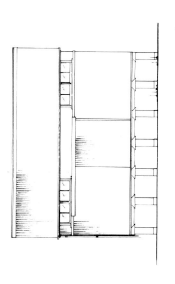

HENLEY GOODS SHED

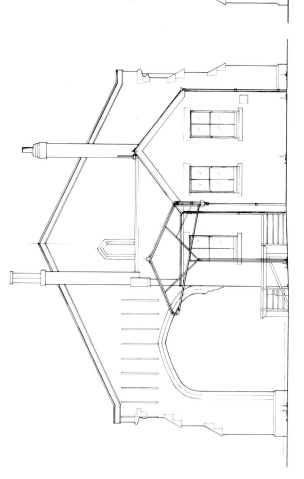

SOUTH END ELEVATION

NORTH END ELEVATION

SCALE – 2 mm to 1 foot

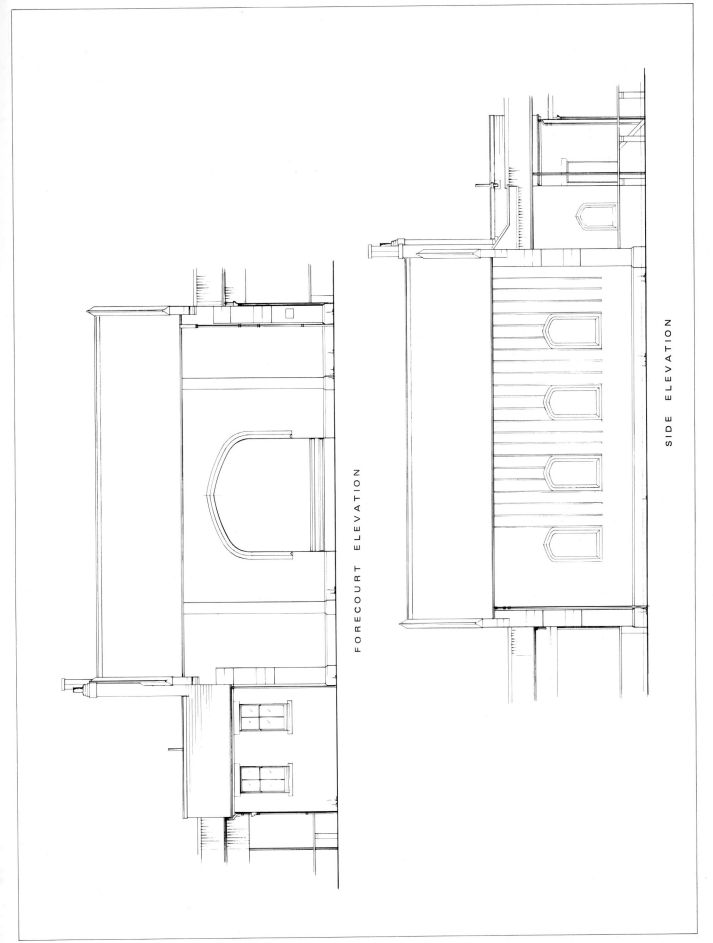

FORECOURT ELEVATION

SIDE ELEVATION

P.W. HUT AT BOLNEY

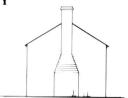
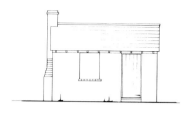
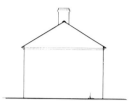
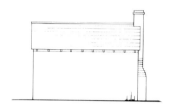

SCALE — 2 mm to 1 foot

MILL LANE SIGNAL BOX

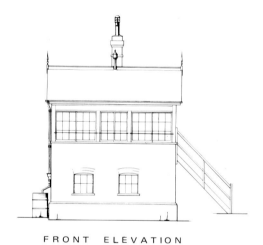

FRONT ELEVATION

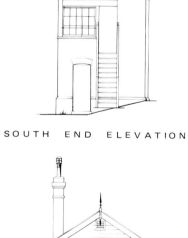

SOUTH END ELEVATION

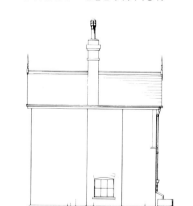

REAR ELEVATION

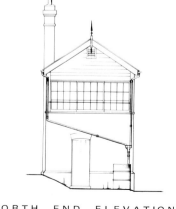

NORTH END ELEVATION

SCALE — 2 mm to 1 foot

LAYOUT DEVELOPMENT AT HENLEY STATION

1876

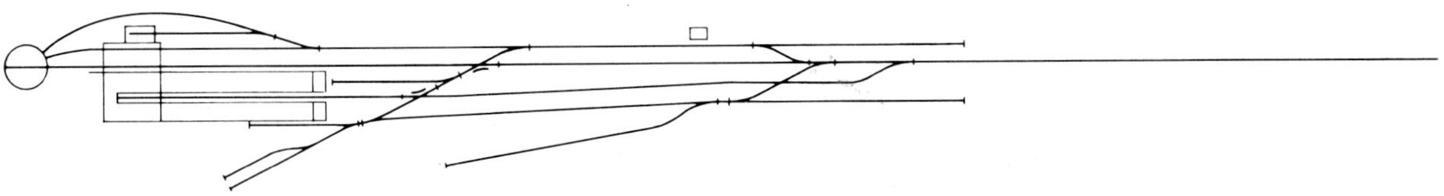

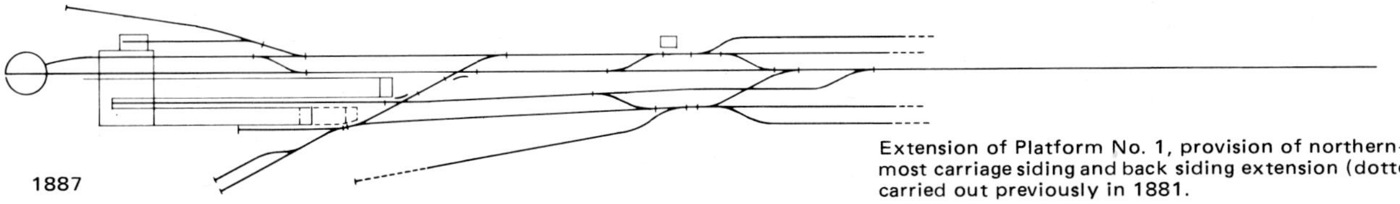

1887

Extension of Platform No. 1, provision of northern-most carriage siding and back siding extension (dotted) carried out previously in 1881.

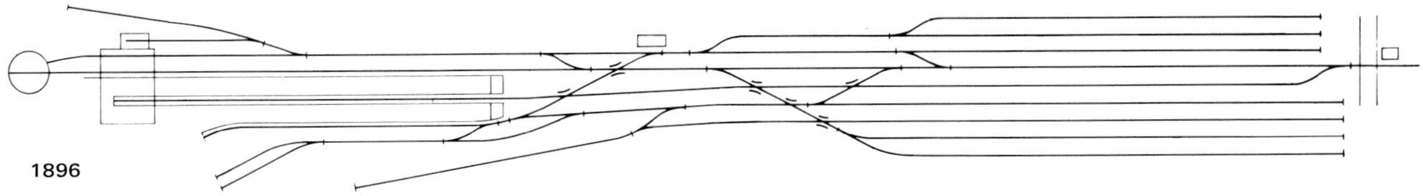

1896

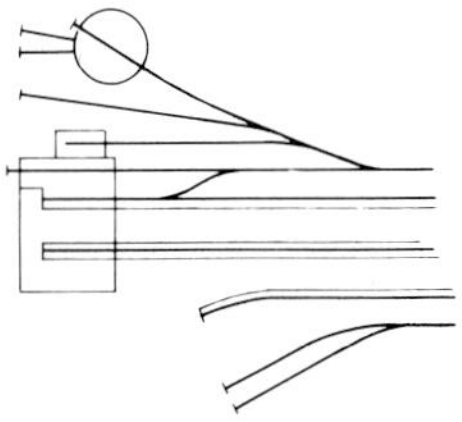

1904

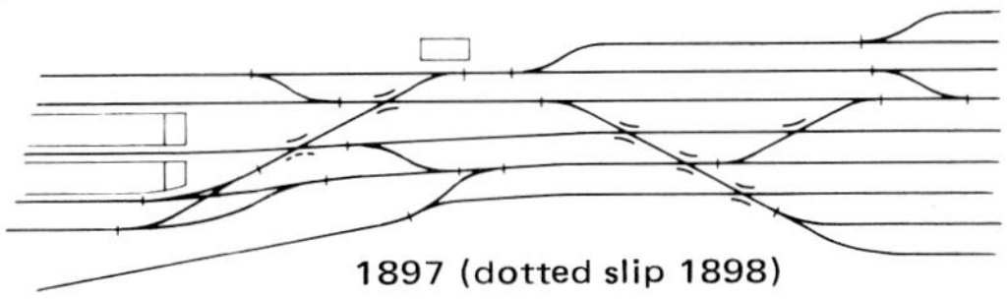

1897 (dotted slip 1898)

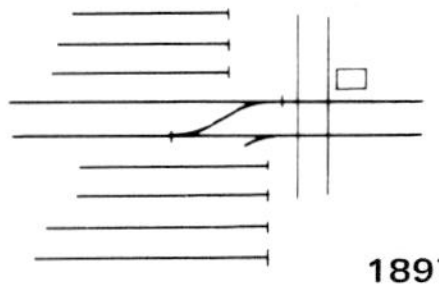

1897

Catchpoint on 'down' running line probably only temporary during construction work.

c.1920 (back siding reconnected in 1904)

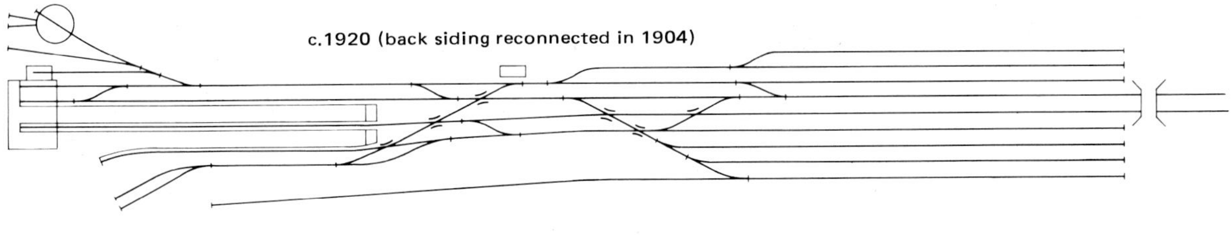

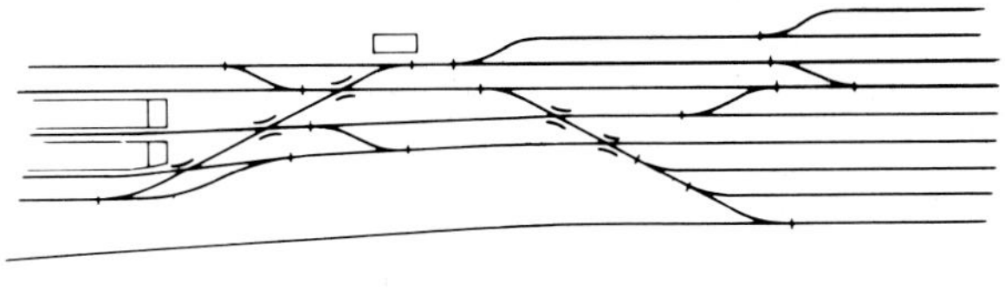

1934

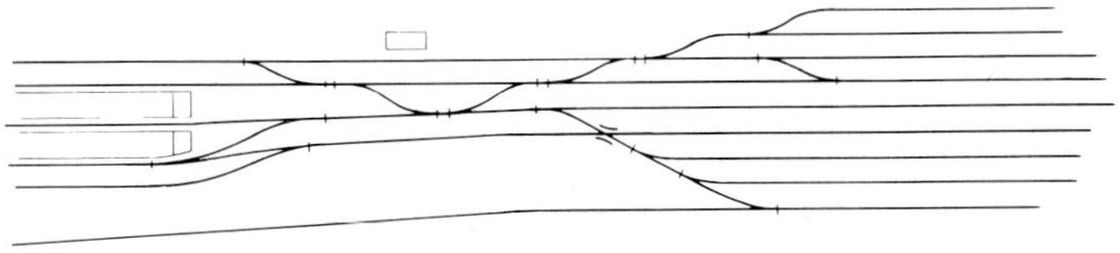

1956

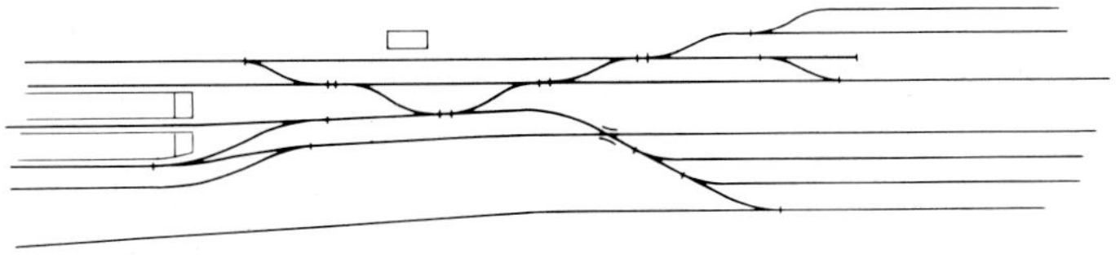

1961

74

SIGNALLING DIAGRAMS

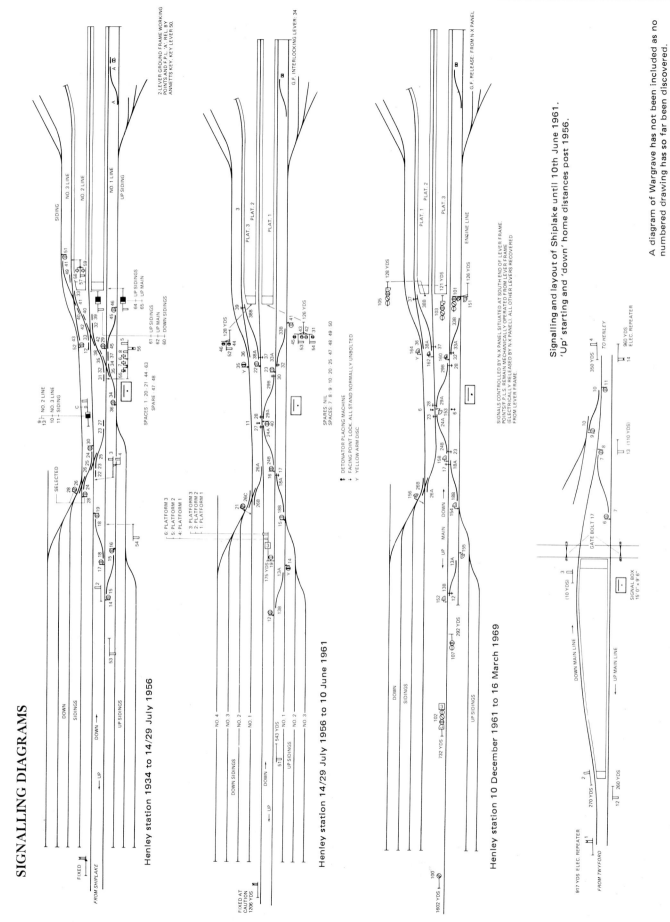

Henley station 1934 to 14/29 July 1956

Henley station 14/29 July 1956 to 10 June 1961

Henley station 10 December 1961 to 16 March 1969

Signalling and layout of Shiplake until 10th June 1961.
'Up' starting and 'down' home distances post 1956.

A diagram of Wargrave has not been included as no numbered drawing has so far been discovered.

LOCOMOTIVES ALLOCATED TO HENLEY

Year	Number	Class	Year	Number	Class	Year	Number	Class
1902	531	'517' class 0—4—2T	1913	4	'Metro' " "	1935	5763	'57XX' " "
	568	'517' " "		5	'Metro' " "		5766	'57XX' " "
	629	'Metro' class 2—4—0T		456	'Metro' " "		9722	'8750' class 0—6—0PT
	639	'633' class 0—6—0T		613	'Metro' " "	1936	4807	'48XX' class 0—4—2T
	972	'Metro' class 2—4—0T		615	'Metro' " "		4809	'48XX' " "
	1471	'517' class 0—4—2T		967	'Metro' " "		4847	'48XX' " "
	3583	'Metro' class 2—4—0T		971	'Metro' " "		4862	'48XX' " "
1903	639	'633' class 0—6—0T		976	'Metro' " "		9722	'8750' class 0—6—0PT
	975	'Metro' class 2—4—0T		1454	'Metro' " "	1937	3715	'8750' " "
	1418	'Metro' " "	1914	4	'Metro' " "		3727	'8750' " "
	1471	'517' class 0—4—2T		456	'Metro' " "		4808	'48XX' class 0—4—2T
1904	5	'Metro' class 2—4—0T		613	'Metro' " "		4842	'48XX' " "
	458	'Metro' " "		615	'Metro' " "		4847	'48XX' " "
	464	'Metro' " "		971	'Metro' " "		4862	'48XX' " "
	467	'Metro' " "	1915	5	'Metro' " "		5766	'57XX' class 0—6—0PT
	613	'Metro' " "		456	'Metro' " "		9791	'8750' class 0—6—0PT
	619	'Metro' " "		613	'Metro' " "	1938	3715	'8750' " "
	639	'633' class 0—6—0T		615	'Metro' " "		3727	'8750' " "
	967	'Metro' class 2—4—0T		971	'Metro' " "		3770	'8750' " "
	968	'Metro' " "	1916	613	'Metro' " "		3783	'8750' " "
	975	'Metro' " "		615	'Metro' " "		4809	'48XX' class 0—4—2T
	976	'Metro' " "		971	'Metro' " "		4817	'48XX' " "
	982	'Metro' " "	1917	613	'Metro' " "		4837	'48XX' " "
	1413	'Metro' " "		615	'Metro' " "	1939	4807	'48XX' " "
	1414	'Metro' " "		971	'Metro' " "		4809	'48XX' " "
	1460	'Metro' " "	1918	613	'Metro' " "		4817	'48XX' " "
1905	5	'Metro' class 2—4—0T		616	'Metro' " "		4842	'48XX' " "
	6	'Metro' " "		1408	'Metro' " "		4862	'48XX' " "
	463	'Metro' " "		1459	'Metro' " "		5762	'57XX' class 0—6—0PT
	464	'Metro' " "	1919	615	'Metro' " "		9722	'8750' class 0—6—0PT
	467	'Metro' " "		616	'Metro' " "	1940	4809	'48XX' class 0—4—2T
	619	'Metro' " "	1920	615	'Metro' " "		4831	'48XX' " "
	967	'Metro' " "		616	'Metro' " "		4837	'48XX' " "
	981	'Metro' " "		1455	'Metro' " "		4847	'48XX' " "
	982	'Metro' " "		1459	'Metro' " "		5772	'57XX' class 0—6—0PT
	983	'Metro' " "	1921	1455	'Metro' " "	1941	3663	'8750' class 0—6—0PT
	986	'Metro' " "		1459	'Metro' " "		4807	'48XX' class 0—4—2T
1906	5	'Metro' " "		1770	'1854' class 0—6—0PT		4825	'48XX' " "
	6	'Metro' " "	1922	615	'Metro' class 2—4—0T		4826	'48XX' " "
	463	'Metro' " "		1459	'Metro' " "		4844	'48XX' " "
	464	'Metro' " "		3242	'3232' class 2—4—0		9773	'8750' class 0—6—0PT
	466	'Metro' " "	1923	615	'Metro' class 2—4—0T	1942	4807	'48XX' class 0—4—2T
	467	'Metro' " "		1406	'Metro' " "		4809	'48XX' " "
	981	'Metro' " "		1459	'Metro' " "		4826	'48XX' " "
	983	'Metro' " "	1924	615	'Metro' " "		4844	'48XX' " "
	1404	'Metro' " "		626	'Metro' " "		4846	'48XX' " "
1907	463	'Metro' " "		1459	'Metro' " "		4847	'48XX' " "
	464	'Metro' " "		3589	'Metro' " "	1943	4807	'48XX' " "
	467	'Metro' " "	1925	615	'Metro' " "		4826	'48XX' " "
	616	'Metro' " "		3589	'Metro' " "		4844	'48XX' " "
	969	'Metro' " "	1927	1459	'Metro' " "		4846	'48XX' " "
	1465	'517' class 0—4—2T	1929	615	'Metro' " "		4847	'48XX' " "
1908	463	'Metro' class 2—4—0T		616	'Metro' " "		5813	'58XX' class 0—4—2T
	464	'Metro' " "		1413	'Metro' " "	1944	3426	'Bulldog' class 4—4—0
	971	'Metro' " "		3610	'36XX' class 2—4—2T		4807	'48XX' class 0—4—2T
	982	'Metro' " "		3614	'36XX' " "		4846	'48XX' " "
1909	464	'Metro' " "	1930	615	'Metro' class 2—4—0T		5813	'58XX' class 0—4—2T
	615	'Metro' " "		616	'Metro' " "	1945	4661	'8750' class 0—6—0PT
	616	'Metro' " "		1430	'517' class 0—4—2T		4847	'48XX' class 0—4—2T
	617	'Metro' " "		2237	'County' class 4—4—2T		5813	'58XX' class 0—4—2T
	971	'Metro' " "	1931	616	'Metro' class 2—4—0T	1946	4661	'8750' class 0—6—0PT
	982	'Metro' " "	1932	1429	'517' class 0—4—2T	1947	3715	'8750' " "
1910	615	'Metro' " "		1880	'1854' class 0—6—0PT		4649	'8750' " "
	967	'Metro' " "		2784	'2721' class 0—6—0PT		5751	'57XX' class 0—6—0PT
	972	'Metro' " "		8721	'8750' class 0—6—0PT		5772	'57XX' " "
	977	'Metro' " "		8740	'8750' " "	1948	4649	'8750' class 0—6—0PT
	982	'Metro' " "		8742	'8750' " "		4661	'8750' " "
1911	967	'Metro' " "	1934	2747	'2721' class 0—6—0PT			
	971	'Metro' " "		5766	'57XX' class 0—6—0PT			
	976	'Metro' " "						
1912	967	'Metro' " "						
	971	'Metro' " "						
	976	'Metro' " "						

ACKNOWLEDGEMENTS

The research for this book has given me immeasurable pleasure and enabled me to continue to enjoy the railway as I choose to remember it, namely in the years prior to 1963. It is a very personal account through which I hope others may share a few memories and discover, as I have, the hitherto unrecorded history.

My research has taken me into the homes of many former staff and their families, each of whom has contributed to the story. In this respect I am particularly indebted to the late Les Babbage who came to Henley as a young fireman from Plymouth Millbay in 1917. He remained on the branch for most of his career and in his retirement spent many hours patiently discussing it with me. I am equally indebted to Reg Daniells, to whom this book is dedicated. In relating his own memories of the branch, particularly in the 1920s, Reg enabled me almost to journey back into an age before I was born. In fact, the combination of images gleaned from both Reg and Les at times almost makes me feel that I have been there with them.

It really is impossible to remember everyone whose kindness over the years has made this book possible, but I would particularly like to mention Chris Turner for his amazing support — as usual all too often at the expense of his own research; Peter Anderson for many leads but in particular for his wide knowledge of local history; Michael Romans for some much needed help with signalling and astute proof checking; Pat Moffatt for so generously putting his own amazing photographs at my disposal; Sean Bolan for so willingly offering his great skill in illustrating those obscure years of the broad gauge; Tony Smith for always being on hand, and Gary Broad for turning up some amazing photographs.

I should also like to thank the following: Austin Attewell, Peter Bartlett, I. D. Beale, Gerry Beale, A. E. Bennett, Ray Bowen, Brakspear's Brewery, Margaret Briggs, Mrs. K. Broadbent, R. J. Buckley, Geo. Bushell & Son, W. A. Camwell, Roger Carpenter, Ted Carpenter, H. C. Casserley, Dave Collins, Jack Crawley, John Crocker, Mrs. Cutbush, Brian Davis, Colin Dawson, M. E. J. Deane, Nick de Courtais, Maurice Earley, John Faulkner, John Finch, the late J. A. Fleming, Stan Fletcher, Pat Garland, W. Y. George, Eddie Goodie, John Harker, Chris Hawkins, Arthur Hearne, John Holton, Chris Hopes, John Hosegood, B. W. Hughes, David Hyde, D. K. Johnson, J. F. Jones, J. S. Jones, Philip J. Kelley, J. E. Kite, Mrs. Lane, Ernest Leaver, Mr. and Mrs. V. G. Mellett, J. H. Meredith, Keith Montague, Eric Mountford, Wendy North, Mike Parsons for his highly valued opinion and advice, P. Pengilley, Photoscript - Deddington, George Reeve, Miss S. Reeves for permission to use her father's photos, R. C. Riley, R. F. Roberts, Royal Photographic Society, J. H. Russell, J. F. Russell-Smith, C. B. Savory, F. I. G. Shaw, Charlie Stone, G. F. Taylor for his patient search in the local library, D. Thompson, Norman Topson, Cliff Tozer, George Trill, Cyril Tristem, Adrian Vaughan, Peter Webber, Les Woods, Brian Wright, Aerofilms, Oxfordshire County Record Office, Public Record Office at Kew, British Railways — in particular M. Hajwa for his incredible patience, David & Charles for the use of L. & G.R.P. photographs, The Henley Standard, and Lens of Sutton.

Finally I must thank my parents for all that they had to put up with through my unfailing enthusiasm in my impressionable youth, and June for loyal support and hard work far beyond the call of duty.